IMAGES
of America

GIRL SCOUT COUNCIL
OF THE
NATION'S CAPITAL

ON THE COVER: The earliest Washington-area Girl Scouts went north to Edgewater, Maryland, for Camp Bradley. The staff for summer 1924 gathered for a group photograph. (Girl Scout Council of the Nation's Capital Archives.)

IMAGES
of America

GIRL SCOUT COUNCIL
OF THE
NATION'S CAPITAL

Ann E. Robertson on behalf of the
Girl Scout Council of the Nation's Capital
Foreword by Gertrude (Bobby) Lerch

ARCADIA
PUBLISHING

Published by Arcadia Publishing
Charleston, South Carolina

Printed in the United States of America

Library of Congress Control Number: 2013937264

For all general information, please contact Arcadia Publishing:
Telephone 843-853-2070
Fax 843-853-0044
E-mail sales@arcadiapublishing.com
For customer service and orders:
Toll-Free 1-888-313-2665

Visit us on the Internet at www.arcadiapublishing.com

This book is dedicated to Juliette Gordon Low and all of the past, present, and future members of her magnificent movement.

CONTENTS

FOREWORD

I joined the Girl Scouts in 1924. It was an opportunity for me to learn new skills and become a part of an amazing sisterhood. When I was a teenager in Ardsley, New York, our founder, Juliette Gordon Low, came to Westchester County, New York, for a countywide rally to "greet the girls and review the troops," a big event for our small village troop! Little did I know then that I would enjoy a lifelong passion for Girl Scouts, spanning nearly nine decades.

Now that I am nearly 104 years young, I reflect on how Girl Scouts has influenced my life. In 1963, I became the president of a newly formed council, the Girl Scout Council of the Nation's Capital, comprising counties in Virginia, Maryland, and the District of Columbia.

Those were difficult times in our country, yet our council, with support from dedicated volunteers, parents, and staff, found ways to bridge racial and socioeconomic divisions to allow girls to be girls! I am so proud that we held our first integrated Girl Scout camps in the summer of 1963. It is one of my greatest achievements.

It is hard to believe that I am older than this organization that I love so dearly. As our council celebrates its 50th anniversary, you will see in the pages that follow our rich history, our proud traditions, and our enduring commitment to girls.

I know the positive impact that Girl Scouts has on our future leaders. Girl Scouts teaches responsibility, leadership, and fellowship.

Together we can achieve more as we soar into the next 100 years of Girl Scouts.

—Gertrude "Bobby" Lerch
President
Girl Scout Council of the Nation's Capital, 1963–1965

ACKNOWLEDGMENTS

Juliette Gordon Low once wrote, "The work of today is the history of tomorrow and we are its makers." But as any historian will tell you, that only holds true if today's work is preserved for future generations.

Girl Scouts is fortunate to have generations of women—and men—who have meticulously saved, preserved, and inventoried the uniforms, handbooks, badges, and more that document our rich heritage. It has been a privilege to join their ranks.

My deepest thanks go to the volunteer members of the Archives and History Committee of the Girl Scout Council of the Nation's Capital: Sandra Alexander, Peter Bielak, Patricia Campbell, Susan Ducey, Florida Fritz, Kathy Seubert, Heberg, Ginger Holinka, Bonnie Johnson, Marva Johnson, Sandy Jones, Julie Lineberry, Joan Paull, Jeana Payne, Mary Rosewater, Amanda Sass, Madeline Tankard, and Virginia Walton, for their warm welcome and enthusiasm for this project.

This project has also been embraced and promoted by the entire council staff, including program services manager Brigid Howe, public relations director Nancy Wood, publications specialist Angela Parsons, public relations writer Deborah Dailey, chief operating officer (COO) Colleen Cibula, chief executive officer (CEO) Lidia Soto-Harmon, and president Diane Tipton.

The majority of the information and images in this collection came from the Girl Scout Council of the Nation's Capital archives, but many longtime leaders also shared their old troop photo albums, including Mary Rose Chappelle, Carol Clanton, Hattie Dorman, Graydon Moss, and Nancy Pearre. Some early images also came from the Library of Congress. Additional assistance came from Anne Bolen, archivist of St. Stephen's and St. Agnes School in Alexandria, Virginia; Pamela Cruz and Yevgeniya Gribov of the Girl Scouts of the USA National Historic Preservation Center; Roberta Dorsch of the Girl Scouts of Central Maryland; and Juliette Gordon Low biographer Stacy A. Cordery of Monmouth College.

Finally, my husband, Mark Bowles, and daughter, Erin Bowles, deserve special thanks for patiently living with a house full of old scrapbooks and clippings, enduring multiple expeditions to the council storage facility, and looking at yet one more wonderful photograph. You have both earned a Girl Scout history badge several times over.

INTRODUCTION

Juliette Gordon Low swept into Washington, DC, in June 1913 on a mission. Just a year earlier, on March 12, 1912, she had launched a new girls' movement with a telephone call to her cousin Nina Anderson Pape: "Come right over, I've got something for the girls of Savannah and all America and all the world and we're going to start it tonight!" Beginning with 18 enthusiastic members in Savannah, Georgia, her hometown, troops popped up across the country, as Low corresponded with hundreds of friends and acquaintances about the benefits of her program. With a national movement underway, she sought to establish a national headquarters in the nation's capital.

Daisy, the nickname Juliette Gordon Low acquired as a child, was a passionate, if unlikely, advocate of the new scouting movement that had begun in Great Britain in 1908. Born on October 31, 1860, she was the daughter of William Washington Gordon II and Eleanor Kinzie Gordon. She grew up in Savannah in a well-to-do family, and her education, with an emphasis on languages, painting, and sculpting, was intended to make her a gracious hostess and wife. She was known as a kind and caring girl who would tend to sick animals and soldiers injured in the Spanish-American War. She was always up for an adventure or mischief, earning her the nickname "Crazy Daisy."

In 1886, she married William "Willy" Mackay Low and followed him to England. The marriage was not happy, as Willy was far more interested in women other than his wife. The couple had no children, and Daisy filled her days with a variety of pursuits. Some followed the conventions of the day, such as travel and being a gracious hostess, but other interests her friends found to be rather odd, such as metalworking and volunteering at a club for poor factory girls in London's Camberwell neighborhood. Willy's death in 1905 freed her to pursue new endeavors.

She met Sir Robert Baden-Powell through mutual friends at a luncheon in May 1911. Baden-Powell had gained fame first as a military officer and then as the author of a series of books and letters on nature observation, tracking prey, camping, and chivalry. His 1908 book *Scouting for Boys* encouraged boys to organize themselves into small units to practice their skills, which hundreds quickly did. Baden-Powell retired from the military in 1910 to focus on his new movement, scouting.

While boys enthusiastically signed up to become Boy Scouts, their sisters came along, too, with some 6,000 trying to register in the group's earliest days. Excluded from the boys' activities, the girls spontaneously organized themselves as "Girl Scouts." In response, Baden-Powell asked his sister Agnes to arrange something for the girls. He opposed the notion of girls joining the Boy Scouts, fearing the girls might become tomboys. Instead, the British female counterpart to Boy Scouting became known as Girl Guiding.

Daisy became enthralled with Baden-Powell's ideas and organized a troop of seven Girl Guides near her summer home in Glen Lyon, Scotland, in the summer of 1911. She launched into a program of knitting and knot tying, cooking, map reading, first aid, and other useful skills balanced with a healthy dose of fun. She returned to London in the fall, organizing two troops there before visiting Savannah in February 1912 and making her famous phone call in March.

The Savannah Girl Guides quickly grew from the 18 girls who gathered on March 12, 1912. Daisy called upon her friends in Savannah society to organize more troops. She even buttonholed Pres. William H. Taft when he visited her parents, and tried to recruit his daughter, Helen.

Daisy returned to England in the fall of 1912, leaving newly appointed executive secretary Edith Johnston in charge. When she returned to Savannah in spring 1913, Daisy discovered that her one troop had grown to six troops in Savannah, and that they had renamed themselves "Girl Scouts."

About the Girl Scout Council of the Nation's Capital

Girl Scouting in the Washington, DC, region has gone by many names over the years, with councils forming, merging, and dissolving many times as part of efforts to better serve girls.

1917   Girl Scout Association of the District of Columbia established.

1924   Girl Scout Association of the District of Columbia formally incorporates in the state of Virginia, and the name is altered to Girl Scouts of the District of Columbia Inc.

1929   Girl Scouts of the District of Columbia divides into six districts.

1935   Prince George's County, Maryland, leaves Girl Scouts of the District of Columbia and establishes the Girl Scouts of Prince George's County.

1939   The city of Alexandria, Virginia, and Arlington County, Virginia, leave Girl Scouts of the District of Columbia and establish the Alexandria Girl Scout Council and the Arlington Girl Scout Council, respectively. The Arlington Girl Scout Council also covered Falls Church, Fairfax City, and Fairfax County.

1940   The Girl Scouts of the District of Columbia begins using the name "Girl Scouts of the District of Columbia and Montgomery County" for clarity but does not formally change its name.

1946   The remaining lone troops in Fairfax County combine into the Fairfax County Council of Girl Scouts.

1957   St. Mary's County, Maryland, joins the Girl Scouts of Prince George's County, which then changes its name to Girl Scouts of Southern Maryland.

1958   Girl Scouts of the District of Columbia changes name to National Capital Girl Scout Council.

1958   The city of Falls Church, Virginia, and the Quantico Marine Corps base schools join the Fairfax County Council of Girl Scouts, and the enlarged council becomes known as the Northern Virginia Girl Scout Council.

1958   Girl Scouts of Frederick County, Maryland, is established as independent council.

1961   Charles County and Calvert County, Maryland, join the Girl Scouts of Southern Maryland.

1962   Girl Scouts of Frederick County, Maryland, joins Baltimore-based Central Maryland Council.

1963   The National Capital, Southern Maryland, Alexandria, Arlington, and Northern Virginia Councils, along with lone troops from Virginia's Prince William, Fauquier, and Loudoun Counties, are combined into the Girl Scout Council of the Nation's Capital.

1963   Four councils merge into the Shawnee Council, based in Cumberland, Maryland. These included the Blue Ridge Council of Virginia, the Eastern Panhandle Council of West Virginia, the Washington County Council of Maryland, and Shawnee, then comprised of Allegany and Garrett Counties in Maryland and Bedford County, Pennsylvania. Shawnee moves its headquarters to Martinsburg, West Virginia, in 1972.

1979   Frederick County, Maryland, switches to the Penn Laurel Girl Scout Council, based in Lancaster, Pennsylvania.

2006   Frederick County, Maryland, joins the Girl Scout Council of the Nation's Capital.

2009   Shawnee Girl Scout Council merges with the Girl Scout Council of the Nation's Capital.

Girl Scout Council of the Nation's Capital
4301 Connecticut Avenue NW
Washington, DC 20008
(202) 237-1670
www.gscnc.org

One

FROM NATIONAL HEADQUARTERS TO NATIONAL CAPITAL

While Girl Scouting began in Savannah and is now based in New York City, Washington, DC, has always been a hub of Girl Scout activity. The first national headquarters was in Washington, two national program centers were located in the area, and the city is the home of the honorary national president, the first lady. Today, it also serves as the place Girl Scouts from across the country gather for major celebrations.

The Girl Scout Council of the Nation's Capital (GSCNC) is one of the two largest councils in the United States, with over 90,000 youth and adult members. It consistently is a top cookie seller and has more girls earning the Gold Award than any other council in the country.

Juliette Gordon Low arrived in Washington, DC, in June 1913, intent on establishing a national headquarters in the nation's capital. She settled on Room 502 of the Munsey Building at 1327 E Street NW. Low hired a part-time secretary to answer mailed inquiries for information and orders for handbooks. Executive secretary Edith Johnston moved from Savannah to Washington, and in July, the movement officially changed its name from Girl Guides to Girl Scouts.

Low paid the rent herself and covered the cost of uniforms, handbooks, and all types of expenses until the organization could become self-funding. She famously sold her wedding pearls in 1914 to raise funds for her girls.

Johnston's first tasks focused on networking and public relations. She traveled to New York to meet the national executive director of the Boy Scouts, James E. West, and made a speech at the YWCA convention in Baltimore. On April 27, 1914, Johnston gave a presentation at the international Congress on the Welfare of the Child in Washington. As troops were organized, Johnston arranged for the Sunday editions of the *Washington Post* and *Washington Star* to run columns in which troops reported their activities. She also coordinated with the American Red Cross to provide first aid training.

The first Washington troop formed in December 1913 under the leadership of Mrs. Giles Scott Rafter, the president of the District of Columbia Congress of Mothers. By June 1914, there were

10 troops in the District of Columbia. Local troops held rallies at Noel Settlement House on February 28, 1914, and Epiphany Church on March 28, 1914. All troops—plus some Boy Scout troops—were invited to an all-day picnic at Wildwood Boy Scout Camp in Takoma Park on May 23, 1914.

The movement began with girls of all socioeconomic levels. Low wrote hundreds of letters to society women she knew from her finishing school days. Many of her peers felt they were too old to go hiking through Rock Creek Park, so they referred her to their daughters and other young women. While many of the first troop captains (leaders) were members of the Junior League, they often worked with troops of very disadvantaged girls. Troop No. 7, for example, was located at the Noel Settlement House, which served some of Washington's poorest residents. Troop No. 7's captain was Martha Bowers, daughter of the US solicitor general. When Martha Bowers married Robert A. Taft, son of President Taft, on October 14, 1914, at St. John's Church in Lafayette Square, her troop sat in the balcony, beaming in their crisp khaki uniforms.

When the national headquarters relocated to New York City in 1916, local leaders had to establish their own organization. Lou Henry Hoover, whose husband Herbert was then head of the US Food Administration, led Troop No. 8 from their home at 2300 S Street NW. An old friend of Low, Lou Henry Hoover agreed to lend her name as acting commissioner for Washington and recruited renowned hostess Henrietta Bates Brooke to found the new council. Brooke and her friend Edith Macy, head of the New York Girl Scouts, invited a dozen Junior League women to tea to view Macy's art collection. Once everyone had arrived, Brooke locked the doors and announced that no one was leaving until they agreed to serve on the board of the new Girl Scout Association of the District of Columbia. Everyone did, and they agreed to start the first troop at the National Cathedral School, where Brooke's daughter Francie was enrolled. The troop's first project was gathering supplies for the Industrial Home School for Children.

On July 17, 1917, the Girl Scout Association of the District of Columbia became the eighth council chartered by the national headquarters. It covered troops in a 25-mile radius, spanning Montgomery County and Prince George's County in Maryland and Arlington County, Fairfax County, and the city of Alexandria in Virginia.

Low also reached out to First Lady Edith Wilson, asking her to become honorary president of the Girl Scouts, as presidents served as honorary presidents of the Boy Scouts of America. Wilson accepted in October 1917, and since then, every first lady has served as honorary national president and welcomed Girl Scouts to the White House for a variety of public and private events. Florence Harding was so pleased to become a Girl Scout that she told a reporter, "I would be perfectly delighted if during my sojourn in the White House, the Girl Scouts would come down there." So many girls did that the national headquarters had to implement a policy of arranging such visits through them.

By 1919, there were 40 active troops and another 23 starting. To handle the workload, Edna Colman, the first commissioner, was hired as director for a salary of $2,000. Bessie Calloway was also hired as a secretary, for $85 per month.

Throughout the 1920s, the Girl Scouts of the District of Columbia worried over money concerns. The council tried a number of fundraising schemes, including operating coffee and teahouses, movies, and even selling *Washington Post* newspaper subscriptions.

The council was formally incorporated in Virginia in 1924, and the name altered to the Girl Scouts of the District of Columbia Inc.

In June 1913, Juliette Gordon Low signed a lease to rent Room 502 of the Munsey Building at 1327 E Street NW for $15 a month. She spent $2 for a sign on the door. National executive secretary Edith Johnston arrived from Savannah and was assisted by Miss McKeever, who was hired to handle mail requests for information, handbooks, and badges. Johnston also publicized troop activities and arranged for local newspapers to publish a regular column about local Girl Scouts. (Harris and Ewing Collection, Library of Congress.)

Washington's Troop No. 1 formed in late 1913 and met weekly at Wilson Normal School. Mrs. Giles Scott Rafter was the leader. The girls picked the sunflower as their patrol symbol and named their cabin in Bradley Hills "Sunflower Lodge." Juliette Gordon Low (right) paid several visits to the troop. The original eight members were Frances Weedon, Evelyn Zane, Elizabeth Gatlin, Elizabeth Falkner, Margaret Conners, Eleanor Putzski, Jessie Bigelow, and Martha Boyle. (Harris and Ewing Collection, Library of Congress.)

Troop No. 2 formed in Capital Heights, Maryland. Juliette Gordon Low had returned to Washington in January 1914 after spending time in England. When she heard that there were girls wanting to start a troop, she set out with executive secretary Edith Johnston to find them. Johnston recalled a dark night in a distant suburb and wading through several feet of snow to find the girls. When they finally arrived, they were very tired and very wet, but Low would not leave until the new troop was properly organized and had planned its next meeting. (Harris and Ewing Collection, Library of Congress.)

Over 250 Washington-area Girl Scouts held a rally at the National Zoo on June 20, 1915. The girls demonstrated the skills and values of Girl Scouting, including this representation of Justice, Liberty, and Peace. The rally coincided with the first National Council Session, and many delegates came to observe the festivities at the zoo.

First Lady Florence Harding (1921–1924) proudly poses in her uniform on the White House portico. She was quite excited to become a Girl Scout, telling visitors, "What I wish is that I were your age and could start life over again as a Girl Scout."

The Little House was built behind the White House in Washington, DC, for the second Better Homes Demonstration Week from June 4–10, 1923. It was a fully working home, with a modern kitchen, breakfast nook, three bedrooms, and a nursery. Between 2,500 and 3,500 people visited daily. After the exhibition, the Better Homes in America and General Federation of Women's Clubs donated it to the Girl Scouts for use as a national training and innovation center. It became the first of many "Little Houses" across the country, where Girl Scouts practiced their homemaking and hospitality skills.

Lou Henry Hoover, wife of the secretary of commerce and national president of the Girl Scouts in 1923, paid for the Little House to be moved from its exhibition site to its new location at 1750 New York Avenue NW, across from the Octagon House. First Lady Grace Coolidge laid the cornerstone. (Harris and Ewing Collection, Library of Congress.)

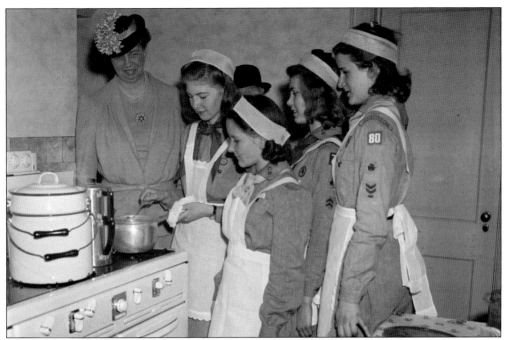

In the 1920s and 1930s, the Little House was the popular place to go on Saturdays. There was always some badge activity to try or new skill to learn, and the first lady, as honorary president of the Girl Scouts, might decide to drop by. These girls are preparing lunch while their guest of honor, Eleanor Roosevelt, observes. (Harris and Ewing Collection, Library of Congress.)

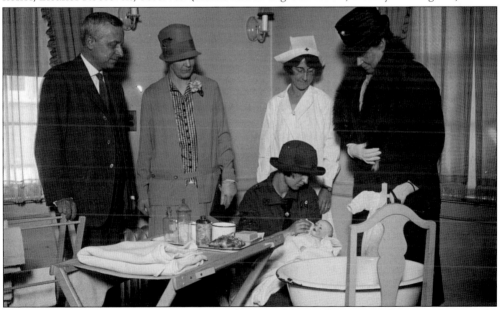

A delegation of Washington dignitaries watches a Girl Scout demonstrate how to take care of a baby. Her audience includes, from to left to right, James Ford, of the Better Homes in America Organization; Mrs. William Jardine, wife of the secretary of agriculture; Miss Stevens, nurse in charge; and Mabel Boardman, secretary of the American Red Cross. (Harris and Ewing Collection, Library of Congress.)

The Girl Scouts of the District of Columbia rented a room in the northwest corner of the second floor of the Little House as its headquarters until 1928, when it outgrew the facility. However, the Little House was still used continuously for training and demonstrations of the domestic arts from June 1923 to April 1945. The building was used as a branch of Girl Scouts of the USA (GSUSA), the national organization, for the next decade and then given to the landowners in May 1955. The Little House was torn down in the early 1970s. There is a commemorative plaque in the lobby of the office building that currently sits at the site. (Harris and Ewing Collection, Library of Congress.)

These are three early leaders of Girl Scouts in Washington, DC. Mary "May" Rebecca Flather, left, was commissioner of the Girl Scouts of the District of Columbia between 1926 and 1928. She donated a house at 1825 M Street NW that was used as council headquarters from 1929 to 1943, and she led the campaign to raise $55,000 to build a permanent camp for Washington Girl Scouts. Camp May Flather opened in Mount Solon, Virginia, in 1930 and remains open today. Standing to the right of First Lady Grace Coolidge, Henrietta Bates Brooke was the first commissioner (president) of the District of Columbia Council and later served as president of the national organization.

One rally was held on the White House lawn on May 15, 1921. Juliette Gordon Low attended and formally invested First Lady Florence Harding as honorary national president. Grace Coolidge (left), wife of then-vice president Calvin Coolidge, reviewed the girls during the rally. (Harris and Ewing Collection, Library of Congress.)

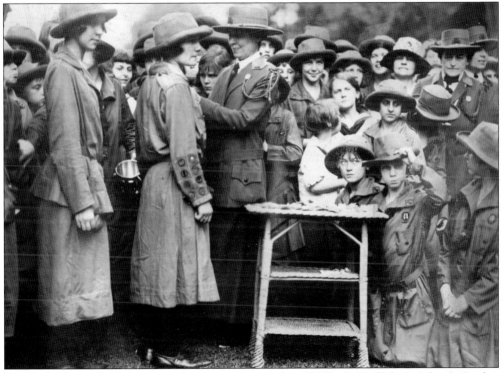

First Lady Grace Coolidge (center) presents an award to Elizabeth Griffith, as Juliette Gordon Low (right, with shoulder cord) watches. Coolidge hosted Girl Scout rallies at the White House, presented awards to girls, and often dropped by the Little House, just a few blocks from the White House.

In 1919, the Girl Scouts of the District of Columbia were allowed to open a "tea and refreshment" stand in East Potomac Park after the park's World War I–era barracks had been replaced by a golf course and picnic sites. A paved road, known as the "Speedway," circled the perimeter of Hains Point, making the park a popular spot for leisurely summer drives. The Girl Scouts opened the Willow Point teahouse in an old streetcar under a large willow tree, with tables on the lawn. Many Washingtonians enjoyed the cool breeze from the water while sipping a glass of cold ginger ale. (National Photo Company Collection, Library of Congress.)

The Willow Point teahouse was such a huge success that in 1922 the Office of Public Buildings and Public Grounds asked Congress for permission to build a larger shelter complete with a "comfort station." The request was approved, and in September 1924, the Girl Scouts moved into their new facility. The classical white pavilion housed a restaurant, snack bar, and restrooms. (Library of Congress.)

Pres. and Mrs. Calvin Coolidge (center) were regular customers at the Willow Point teahouse, as were their predecessors, Pres. and Mrs. Warren G. Harding. Girls working at the house took extra care with their khaki uniforms in case they were lucky enough to wait on a famous customer. When the Hardings stopped by one day in June 1921, their waitress carefully preserved a slice of cake the president had left behind, only to have her little brother gobble up her souvenir once she got home. (National Photo Company Collection, Library of Congress.)

Congress restructured park management in 1925, and the park's director, Lt. Col. U.S. Grant III, informed the Girl Scouts that their concession would expire on December 31, 1925. The park service operated the restaurant until 1962, when it became a visitor's center and, later, office space. The building fell into disrepair and was razed in 1987, shortly after this photograph was taken. (Library of Congress.)

First Lady Grace Coolidge formally opened a second teahouse at Peirce Mill in Rock Creek Park on November 16, 1921. The mill had housed a restaurant before, but the Girl Scouts redecorated it with pale yellow walls, blue tables and chairs, yellow curtains trimmed with blue fringe, and yellow and blue candles on each table. Menu favorites included coffee, muffins with marmalade, waffles with maple syrup, and gingerbread. Though not a financial success, the council continued to use Peirce Mill for meetings and training sessions. Peirce Mill is located less than one mile from the current Nation's Capital main office at 4301 Connecticut Avenue NW. (National Photo Company Collection, Library of Congress.)

Evalina Gleaves, daughter of Rear Admiral Albert Gleaves, served as council director from 1924 to 1926. Under her leadership, membership grew from 666 girls to 1,144. Gleaves was selected to be a delegate to the World Conference at Foxlease, England, in July 1924. She left her post to marry Benjamin Cohen, and more than 400 Girl Scouts attended the wedding.

Lou Henry Hoover, shown visiting the Little House on May 16, 1925, was a great friend of Girl Scouts in general, especially in Washington. She served as acting commissioner of the fledgling Girl Scouts of the District of Columbia (1917–1918), national president (1922–1925 and 1935–1937), and honorary national president while first lady (1929–1933). She also led Washington's Troop No. 8 in the 1920s and hosted meetings, such as the February 4, 1930, council meeting, at the White House. (National Photo Company Collection, Library of Congress.)

England's prime minister Ramsay MacDonald visited the White House in October 1929. When Lou Hoover learned that his daughter Ishbel was a Girl Guide, she immediately invited local Girl Scouts to come to the White House to greet them. (Harris and Ewing Collection, Library of Congress.)

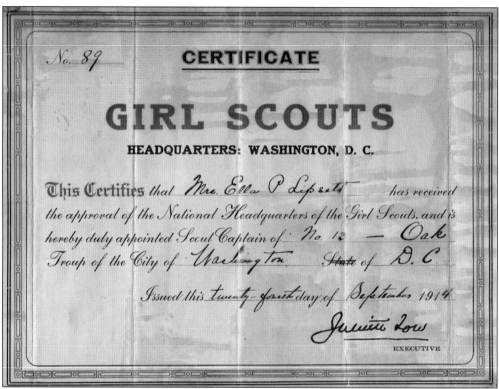

CERTIFICATE

No. 89

GIRL SCOUTS

HEADQUARTERS: WASHINGTON, D. C.

This Certifies that *Mrs. Ella P. Lipsett* has received the approval of the National Headquarters of the Girl Scouts, and is hereby duly appointed Scout Captain of: *No 13 — Oak* Troop of the City of *Washington* State of *D. C.*

Issued this *twenty-fourth* day of *September* 1914

Juliette Low

EXECUTIVE

THE **FESTIVAL of NATIONS**

AUSPICES OF
The GIRL SCOUTS
OF THE
DISTRICT OF COLUMBIA INCORPORATED
A GREAT SPRING FESTIVAL AND
INTERNATIONAL SPECTACLE

Ella P. Lipsett was appointed captain (leader) of Troop No. 13 on September 24, 1914. Her appointment certificate, the 89th issued, also indicates that her troop chose the oak as its troop crest. By 1916, the troop had divided into two patrols, one led by Katherine Gibbs and the other by Minnie Jones. Mrs. H.A. Haffey was the leader.

From April 27 to May 2, 1931, the council sponsored the Festival of Nations, an enormous pageant and fundraiser at Constitution Hall. Girls performed songs and dances representing the cultures of Mexico, Czechoslovakia, Canada, and Japan to an audience made up of fellow Girl Scouts, families, and members of the diplomatic corps. The event got off to a rough start when chickens brought on stage to represent a Mexican cockfight got out of control, especially as cockfighting was illegal in the District of Columbia. While the festival was highly successful in terms of publicity, the council struggled to pay all of the expenses incurred.

Two

GIRL SCOUT WAYS

While uniforms, badges, and age levels have changed over the years, the core principles of Girl Scouting remain the same—skills, service, and leadership. Troops, activities, and trips are girl-led, with trusted adults providing guidance as needed.

Today's Girl Scouts are divided into the following six age levels: Daisies (kindergarten and first grade), Brownies (second and third grades), Juniors (fourth and fifth grades), Cadettes (sixth through eighth grades), Seniors (ninth and 10th grades), and Ambassadors (11th and 12th grades).

Girl Scouts are organized into troops; troops combine to form service units (usually based on one high school and its feeder schools); and service units combine to form associations (usually two to three associations per county). Events held at the service unit or association level bring together girls of different ages, schools, and backgrounds and help them understand that they are part of a much larger sisterhood.

Activities are planned around the principle of progression. As girls grow, they take on increasingly more complex tasks. Daisies, for example, may spend a day at camp but return home at night. Brownies might spend one night in a lodge, while Juniors spend a weekend in a glen shelter, and Cadettes pitch tents during backpacking trips.

In the early days of Girl Scouting, girls progressed from Tenderfoot scouts to Second Class and First Class rank as they passed skills tests. All girls—and often adults—began at the Tenderfoot level, whatever their age. But increasingly girls rejected this structure, as new Girl Scouts wanted to be with girls their own age. In response, GSUSA restructured the program in 1963 with skills and badges defined by age level, not cumulatively by years in Scouting.

Juliette Gordon Low reached out to the community to educate her girls. She had an early partnership with the Red Cross to learn first aid skills, and the District of Columbia Council negotiated a deal with the local schools to apply schoolwork toward badge requirements. Washington-area troops drew on local experts to administer proficiency tests for badges. For her bird finder badge, 14-year-old Effie Wade Dean went down to the Smithsonian Institution, where its bird expert asked her to identify the stuffed birds in his office.

Girl Scout councils provide a wealth of training opportunities for adult volunteers at little or no cost. All adults are required to take a basic "intro to Girl Scouts" course, as well as focused training on the particular age level for their troop. The trainings are conducted either in person by experienced volunteers or online, with scheduled telephone conference calls. Once the basics are mastered, adults can take additional instruction for camping, backpacking, archery, kayaking, songs, ceremonies, crafts, first aid and CPR, specific girl awards, troop finances, troop travel (domestic and foreign), international Girl Scouting, knots, scrapbooking, cooking with Girl

Scout cookies, and more. Adults managing cookie sales, running day camps, or other events also receive specialized training at no cost.

The highest award in Girl Scouting has also changed over time. The Golden Eagle of Merit, introduced in 1916, was renamed the Golden Eaglet in 1919. The Curved Bar was introduced in 1940 but was then replaced by First Class in 1963. The entire Girl Scout curriculum was revised in 1980, with new badges and awards for each age level. The Silver Award replaced First Class as the highest award for Cadettes, and the Gold Award was introduced in 1980 as the highest honor for Girl Scout Seniors and Ambassadors. The GSUSA board of directors resolved in 1996 to never change the name of the highest award again.

The Girl Scout Leadership Experience was introduced in 2008 to develop three aspects of leadership: discover, connect, and take action. Girls take Journeys—a series of activities around the themes of social change, the environment, and storytelling—that culminate in Take Action Projects that make the world a better place.

All Girl Scouts, young and old, female and male, make the same promise and recite the same laws, which outline the principles of Girl Scouts:

The Girl Scout Promise

On my honor, I will try:
To serve God and my country,
To help people at all times,
And to live by the Girl Scout Law.

The Girl Scout Law

I will do my best to be
honest and fair,
friendly and helpful,
considerate and caring,
courageous and strong, and
responsible for what I say and do,
and to
respect myself and others,
respect authority,
use resources wisely,
make the world a better place, and
be a sister to every Girl Scout.

The Daisy program was introduced nationwide for kindergarteners in 1984 and takes its name from Juliette Gordon Low's childhood nickname. Program changes in 2008 expanded Daisies to include first graders, offered vests instead of tunics, and allowed them to sell cookies for the first time in 2009. These Daisies attended the Nation's Capital Inter-Faith Service at Washington National Cathedral on April 28, 2012.

The first American Brownie Pow-Wow was held at the Manor Club in Norbeck, Maryland, in November 1922 and was organized by Edith Blair Staton. Participants agreed that Brownie "packs" (troops) should be divided into groups of six girls and led by adult Brown Owls (leaders). These Brownies and their older Girl Scout friends are practicing their camping skills at the home of Lou Henry Hoover in 1918. (Harris and Ewing Collection, Library of Congress.)

The Brownie Investiture ceremony has not changed in decades. A girl is twirled around by her leader or troop member and then leans over to look into a "pond"—usually a mirror—saying, "Twist me, and turn me, and show me the elf. I looked in the water and saw . . . myself!" Only then can she recite the Brownie Promise.

The year 1963 brought many changes to Girl Scouting. The Intermediate level was divided into Juniors (ages 9–11) and Cadettes (12–14), and new handbooks were introduced for all four levels. Girls across the country mobilized on September 11, 1963, to deliver handbooks to members of Congress. From left to right, Senior Mary Knight, Cadette Carol Gore, Junior Marsha Blosser, and Brownie Rebecca Ebend of Winchester, Virginia, are all ready for meetings with their new handbooks.

While Intermediates progressed in rank from Tenderfoot to Second Class, then First Class, and finally Curved Bar as they accumulated skills and badges, Juniors earned the Sign of the Arrow and Sign of the Star. Washington, DC, Junior Troop No. 1466 models Junior uniforms from the 1960s and 1970s. The young lady in the first row, second from left, has earned both signs and has sewn them above her Brownie Wings. (Courtesy of Hattie Dorman.)

By the time girls reach the Cadette, Senior, and more recent Ambassador levels, they may have saved up enough cookie money to travel. Washington, DC, Senior Troop No. 1027 sailed to Europe aboard the *Queen Mary* in 1965 to visit Our Chalet, the world center in Switzerland. They also visited Our Cabaña, the world center in Mexico, on a separate trip.

The Senior program has always emphasized career exploration. In the 1950s, Seniors could earn child care, library, museum, occupational therapy, office, program, and ranger service bars. More fields were added over time, and the Southern Maryland Council developed a Public Relations Girl Scout program that was adopted nationally in 1962. Members of Forest Heights, Maryland, Senior Troop No. 15 received their public relations aide pins from Mrs. Paul Egli in 1959.

The Mariner Girl Scout program was introduced in the 1930s for girls aged 15 and older. Mariner troops focused on water safety, knots, weather, navigation, boat care, and emergency procedures. Given the many rivers and the Chesapeake Bay in the region, the Mariner program was very popular in the Washington, DC, area. In June 1941, 19 Mariners and three adult skippers from the District of Columbia sailed the three-masted schooner *William J. Stanford* from Annapolis to Solomon's Island, Maryland, and back, stopping at the Chesapeake Bay Marine Laboratory, the State House at St. Mary's City, and Fort McHenry. The trip took 10 days.

Juliette Gordon Low learned how to fly an airplane, and one of the first badges for Girl Scouts encouraged them to learn the skill as well. Other teens followed her lead, and by 1941, the Wing Scout program for Seniors created troops that specialized in aviation skills. Here, Wing Scouts from Washington, DC, Troop No. 492 pose before their flight leaves for a New York City sightseeing trip in 1956. (Girl Scouts of the USA National Historic Preservation Center. Used by permission.)

Girls can earn badges in a range of topics, like camping, cooking, child care, bugs, digital photography, and web design. Badges, pins, and other recognitions are presented at a Court of Awards ceremony, where girls can share their new skills with their families.

Ceremonies, like all Girl Scout activities, are supposed to be girl-led. Even the youngest girls can pick a song to sing, recite the Promise, and make simple decorations. The ceremony does not have to be perfect—it just has to be theirs. Lois Bell, Nation's Capital president from 1987 to 1993, helps two girls light candles to begin a solemn ceremony marking the 80th birthday of Girl Scouts in 1992.

Eleanor Putzski of District of Columbia Troop No. 1 wears the Golden Eagle of Merit, pinned just below her Sunflower Patrol crest. Eleanor was named "Best Girl Scout in America" in 1918 and received her Eagle from First Lady Edith Wilson at a ceremony at the White House. The award was the highest available from 1916 to 1919 and required earning 14 proficiency badges; Eleanor earned 25. Fewer than 50 Golden Eagles of Merit were presented before the honor was revised and renamed the Golden Eaglet. (Harris and Ewing Collection, Library of Congress.)

Today, the highest earned award is the Gold Award. Recipients must complete a sustainable leadership project that takes 80 hours. With some 200 Gold Awards presented each year, Nation's Capital consistently has more Gold Award recipients than any other council in the country. Teens can also earn the council's prestigious Silver Trefoil Award, which requires 100 additional hours of service in a variety of categories. Currently recipients are recognized at the "In Your Honor" ceremony held at Trinity Washington University. Jan Verhage (GSCNC CEO 1985–2010) (left) and current council president Diane Tipton pose with the highly decorated ladies of Troop No. 2016.

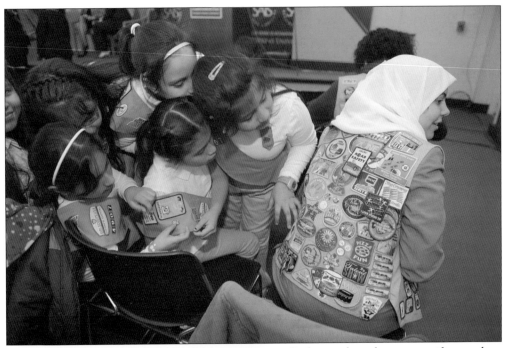

Badges and patches turn uniform sashes and vests into a wearable scrapbook, as each new addition commemorates an event or new skill. Younger girls love to check out the patches on an older girl's vest and plan what they want to do as they continue in Girl Scouting. Abrar Omeish, right, a girl member of the Nation's Capital board of directors, has plenty of experiences to inspire them.

Adults like their patches, too. Many adults display their accumulated patches on blankets, tablecloths, or tote bags. Jean Porter was always easy to recognize with her colorful patch jacket.

Thinking Day connects Girl Scouts in the United States with Girl Guides, their counterparts around the world. Individual troops pick a country and study their culture, food, music, and scouting traditions. All the troops in a town or county then come together to share what they have learned. Thinking Day is held on February 22, the birthday of both Sir Robert Baden-Powell, the founder of Boy Scouts, and his wife, Olave Baden-Powell.

Lillian B. Mountford of Arlington, Virginia, was an enthusiastic supporter of the Juliette Low World Friendship Fund, which promotes international friendship through service projects, training events, and exchange visits to the four world centers. Mountford sponsored a Juliette Low Rally in 1945 at Lubber Run Park in Arlington, Virginia.

Girl Scouts love to try out the uniforms that their mothers—or grandmothers—wore. Takoma Park Troop No. 118 put on a fashion show of vintage uniforms in 1963. Today, the 1963 uniforms are considered vintage.

And a few veteran Girl Scouts can still fit into their own old uniforms, including Mariner Karen Brown (left) and Girl Scout historian Alma Knox, wearing her uniform from the 1920s.

Girls learn about citizenship, patriotism, and service to their country when they learn how to perform a flag ceremony. Members of the color guard must maintain the same level of dignity whether they are posting the colors at a local shopping mall or on the National Mall.

The largest regular gatherings for Girl Scouts are the National Council Sessions, now held every three years. Washington hosted the ninth National Council Session, at the Wardman Park Hotel, April 24–27, 1923. At the time of the meeting, Girl Scouting was gaining 10,000 new members each month. (Harris and Ewing Collection, Library of Congress.)

Nation's Capital's girl delegates to the National Council Session in Houston, Texas, in November 2011 are ready to Rock the Mall to celebrate the Girl Scout centennial in 2012. The National Council Session sets policies for the national Girl Scout organization, and any registered girl age 14 or above is eligible to be a voting delegate at both the national meeting and their own council's annual meeting. Over 1,000 Seniors and Ambassadors from across the country attended a special Girl Scout Leadership Institute ahead of the 2011 National Council Session.

Girl Scout cookies have been around almost as long as Girl Scouts. The cookie program teaches decision making, goal setting, money management, people skills, and business ethics. Nation's Capital is one of the largest selling councils in the country, selling 4.5 million boxes in 2013. The council became the first member of the Million Dollar Club in 1986, when cookie sale profits amounted to over $1 million.

Local television newswoman J.C. Hayward, left, served as honorary chair of the annual cookie program from 1971 to 1982. Here, she joins council president Lynn Heebner and a group of girls ready to deliver cookies.

The first Girl Scout Week was held from October 25 to November 1, 1919, and coincided with Juliette Gordon Low's birthday on October 31. In 1953, the National Council Session voted to move the celebration to March, to commemorate the first troop meeting on March 12, 1912. From 1977 to 1997, Springfield Mall in Virginia was the site of "Girl Scouts in Action," a week of concerts, displays, and other events celebrating Girl Scouting.

In 2006, Junior Troop No. 1272 of Leesburg, Virginia, celebrated Juliette Gordon Low's birthday with a camping trip to Potomac Woods. They made cupcakes, sang "Happy Birthday," and had a Scouts' Own ceremony.

Parades are popular patriotic activities for troops. Troop No. 677 explained the Bill of Rights in Alexandria, Virginia, for a parade in honor of George Washington's birthday in February 1990. Alexandria is also home to Washington's estate, Mount Vernon, which offers special programs for Girl Scouts throughout the year.

Junior Troop No. 1790 of Leonardtown, Maryland, won first place in the 2006 St. Mary's County Fair Parade for its float and enthusiastic Girl Scout singing. The county's individual troops combined with those in Prince George's County to form the Southern Maryland Council in 1957.

Troops are required to have an adult volunteer who has passed a basic first aid course, as well as CPR training for both children and adults. James Sherman conducted a first aid course for leaders from Langley Park, Maryland, in January 1955. From left to right are Sherman, patient Shirley Bell, Mrs. Devido, Ruth Thomas, Mary Berstine, Sunny Freedmon, and Jennie Willett.

Juliette Gordon Low teamed with the Red Cross to provide basic first aid training for girls and adults. Girls particularly like to give demonstrations of their first aid skills. The annual rallies held at the Washington National Zoo in the 1920s featured many presentations in which a troop member would dramatically "faint" or "break" her ankle. The rest of the troop would then rush in to provide expert assistance.

Each Girl Scout year culminates in a bridging ceremony, where girls advance to the next level. Girls prepare for the transition by visiting an older troop or trying out one of their badges and by hosting younger girls moving up to their level. The bridging process reinforces the continuity of the program and makes sure girls have familiar, friendly faces waiting for them in their new troops and, often, their new schools.

One of the first activities any Brownie does is to make a sit-upon—a waterproof cushion to use during troop meetings, field trips, and camping. Brownies learn how to make sit-upons and s'mores as a part of earning their Girl Scout Ways badge.

Ten members of Senior Troop No. 53 of University Park, Maryland, reunited in September 2006 at Big Meadows Lodge on Skyline Drive in Virginia, near their favorite troop campsite, Rock Spring Shelter. Many had not seen each other for 57 years. They traded stories about their leader, Mrs. Harry Hart, and some of the "girls" even brought their old uniforms.

SWAPS (sentimental whatchamacallits affectionately pinned somewhere) are small pieces of art attached to a hat or shirt with a safety pin. Troops make SWAPS with a theme, such as cherry blossoms, and trade them with other troops. The giant sing-a-longs on the National Mall are great places to swap.

Generations of Washington-area Girl Scouts were fortunate to have a direct link to founder Juliette Gordon Low. Marian Corbin Aslakson, center, was a member of Low's original troop in Savannah. Aslakson lived in Bethesda, Maryland, for many years and generously shared her stories and love of Girl Scouting. She was a vigorous campaigner to save Rockwood National Center, donating a dozen sterling silver goblets to be auctioned off to raise funds for the legal fight.

Adults are also recognized for their service. The Knox Award, introduced in 1988, recognizes individuals whose continuous service to the Girl Scout Council of the Nation's Capital exemplifies the spirit, dedication, and enjoyment of Girl Scouting and the principles of Juliette Gordon Low's movement. The award honors Lucy Knox (seated), Irene Knox (standing), and their sister-in-law Alma (pictured on page 36). These three women were among the first Girl Scouts in the Washington area and remained active throughout their lives.

The Nation's Capital Archives and History Committee was formed in 1983 to preserve the history of the council. That task was immensely helped by the work of two women, Alma Lauxman Knox (left) and Virginia Hammerley (right). The two women joined Troop No. 12 in the mid-1920s and worked as counselors at Camp May Flather in the 1930s. Knox was an original member of the Archives Committee and compiled volumes of information about the early days of Girl Scouting in the Washington area. Hammerley became a staff member of the District of Columbia council and left five thick scrapbooks of photographs, clippings, and memories. This book would have been impossible without their legacy.

At the April 2013 Nation's Capital Annual Meeting, members of the Archives and History Committee received a donation of badges and a copy of Juliette Gordon Low's 1914 application to patent the trefoil design. From left to right are Ginger Holinka, Sandra Alexander, Bonnie Johnson, Nation's Capital chief executive officer Lidia Soto-Harmon, Amanda Sass, Ann Robertson, Mary Rosewater, Nation's Capital president Diane Tipton, Madeline Tankard, Kathy Seubert Heberg, Jeana Payne, and Peter Bielak, with Chevy. Not pictured are Patricia Campbell, Susan Ducey, Florida Fritz, Marva Johnson, Sandy Jones, Julie Lineberry, Joan Paull, and Virginia Walton.

Three

COUNCILS LARGE
AND SMALL

Washingtonians began to migrate to the suburbs in the 1930s, and Girl Scouts grew and reorganized to meet the changing needs of girls and their families. More and more girls wanted to join troops, including girls from minority groups. Council staff struggled to meet the demand for more troops spread further apart at a time when the Great Depression meant smaller and smaller budgets.

The District of Columbia Council divided its jurisdiction into districts in 1929; roughly each county was a separate district. This put increased responsibility on the volunteer committees recruiting leaders. While this helped somewhat in terms of staff responsibilities, services became uneven and differed from district to district. At the Washington office's suggestion, the Prince George's County, Maryland, district became the independent Girl Scouts of Prince George's County in 1935. Jessie Dashiell, the DC Council's field captain for the county, became the council's first commissioner.

The departure of Prince George's County did little to reduce Washington's workload. In October 1939, Dorothy Davidson, the director of the DC Council, announced that no new troops would be registered until funding became available to hire more staff.

Money was a constant worry for the local Girl Scouts. After the initial start-up of the Washington Council, benefactors tired of paying out of their pockets for expenses. The year 1929 brought a major victory, when the council qualified for Community Chest funds. Now known as the United Way, the Community Chest collected donations from local businesses and redistributed them to community groups.

But that exciting development did not mean financial security, as the Depression meant fewer donations going into the Community Chest and more girls needing financial aid to attend camp. In 1934, the Community Chest slashed its donation to the Girl Scouts by one-third, and Washington had to borrow money to pay its national dues. Fewer campers signed up for Camp May Flather, leaving the council in debt following the 1935 camping season. In response, the Community Chest gave permission for the first local cookie sale, which was held in March 1936.

Juliette Gordon Low's commitment to make Girl Scouting available to all girls was put to the test as African American girls asked to form troops, too. At the 1929 National Council Session in New Orleans, Girl Scouts of the USA voted to allow African American troops to officially register, after many had informally organized across the country. While some accounts identify the first such local troop as Troop No. 9 of Hyattsville, Maryland, in 1930, many longtime Washington-area Girl Scouts vividly remember an African American troop that began in North Brentwood in 1926.

In March 1934, the DC Council appointed Virginia McGuire to head District VII, a new district exclusively for African American troops. By 1941, District VII had 21 troops and 500 registered girls.

Pine Crest, a day camp for African American girls, began in the summer of 1937 with a $600 grant from the Community Chest. On visitor's day during the 1939 session, a representative of the Daughters of the American Revolution went to the camp, located at Benning Road and Minnesota Avenue NE in Washington, to present an American flag to the camp and give a presentation on flag etiquette.

By 1936, there were only three troops based in Washington's Catholic churches. Rev. Edward A. Fuller contacted the council about organizing troops at the Church of St. Aloysius. Fuller proposed his own investiture ceremony, which the council rejected as being too Catholic.

The Girl Scouts also insisted that the Washington Archdiocese would need to help pay for an additional staff member to handle the expected high demand for new troops. Without such funds, Davidson refused Father Fuller's request to register an African American troop. The priest turned to New York, asking if he could register directly with the national office. A tug-of-war ensued between the Washington and New York offices, with both insisting the issues involved were staffing, budget, and autonomy, not race. Ultimately, Fuller's troop was recognized as a less formal "Girl Scout Club," and Eleanor Durrett replaced Davidson as the local director.

Over the years, the council changed shape several times to improve local governance and efficiency. Prince George's County, Maryland, became a separate council in 1935 and then changed its name to Girl Scouts of Southern Maryland when St. Mary's County joined the council in 1957. Charles and Calvert County Girl Scouts joined the council in 1961. The Washington Council began using the name "Girl Scouts of the District of Columbia and Montgomery County" for clarity, but did not formally change its name until 1958, when it became the National Capital Council.

Two new councils emerged in Northern Virginia in 1939, the Alexandria Council in the city of Alexandria and the Arlington Girl Scout Council in nearby Arlington County. The Arlington Council also covered Falls Church, Fairfax City, and Fairfax County. Eight years later, in 1946, the remaining lone troops in Fairfax County combined into the Fairfax County Council of Girl Scouts. That council expanded in 1958 to encompass Falls Church and the Quantico Marine Corps base schools, and the larger council became known as the Northern Virginia Girl Scout Council.

In 1946, GSUSA launched the Green Umbrella (or Council Coverage) campaign, a multiyear process that reduced the number of councils from 3,000 to 1,000. While the reorganization streamlined operations and brought new programming opportunities, many merged councils were sad to see the names of their legacy councils removed from signs, camps, and sashes.

For Girl Scouts in the Washington, DC, region, realignment meant a return to the 1930s council boundaries. In 1963, the National Capital, Southern Maryland, Alexandria, Arlington, and Northern Virginia Councils, along with lone troops in Virginia's Prince William, Fauquier, and Loudoun Counties, were combined into the Girl Scout Council of the Nation's Capital.

Farther west in 1963, four councils merged into the Shawnee Council, based in Cumberland, Maryland. These included the Blue Ridge Council of Virginia, the Eastern Panhandle Council of West Virginia, the Washington County Council of Maryland, and Shawnee, then comprised of Allegany and Garrett Counties in Maryland and Bedford County, Pennsylvania. Shawnee moved its headquarters to Martinsburg, West Virginia, in 1972.

Frederick County, Maryland, organized as an independent council in 1958 and then joined the Baltimore-based Central Maryland Council in 1962. It switched to the Penn Laurel Girl Scout Council in 1979.

The national organization voted in favor of starting African American troops at its national convention in 1929. The Washington area had already made that change. Founded in 1924, Troop No. 66 of North Brentwood, Maryland, was one of the first troops for African American girls. Myrtle Davis Maynard, a member of Troop No. 66, fondly remembered her leader, Nellie P. Moss, pictured here. "She has special plans for her girls, such as wonderful meetings, demonstration cooking classes, drama, vacations at Carr's Beach near Annapolis, oratorical contests, lessons in cleanliness, dances at the club house and of course camping. Most of all her insistence on the importance of education."

Dorothy Greene led the Girl Scouts of the District of Columbia from 1926 to 1932. As the first director of Camp May Flather, she earned praise for enlisting the support and skills of the local population. She left the Girl Scout council in 1932 to launch Bear Trap Farm, a retreat near the camp. When Greene was killed in an automobile accident in 1943, the council issued a moving tribute to her memory and delivered it to her family and to her close friend and partner, Lillian E. Smith.

The Prince George's County, Maryland, district launched Camp Thorn in 1933. The day camp was located in College Park, Maryland, and cost $2 for an entire summer of fun. Before it could open, however, Girl Scouts had to renovate the existing cabin. Jessie Dashiell, who became the first commissioner of the independent Prince George's Council in 1935, nails a sign on the spruced-up cabin.

The new Arlington Council initially sent girls to Camp Chopowamsic, a National Parks Service facility in Triangle, Virginia, before purchasing land for Camp Potomac Woods in 1942. Commissioner Mrs. Raymond Sawyer and her husband supervise development at Potomac Woods before the first camp session.

Virginia McGuire was named the organizer for District VII, the African American division, in 1934, and later became the first African American member of the council's governing board. In 1959, the administration building at Camp May Flather was named in her honor. This photograph was rescued from the camp dining hall after a roof leak in 1942.

In 1934, Lelia Scott Thomas and Henrietta Green formed the first Brownie and Girl Scout troops for African American girls in the District of Columbia at the Dunbar Recreation Center. More troops followed, and in 1944, Ethel Harvey began a Brownie troop at Metropolitan Baptist Church in Washington. She led many thriving troops, including Troop No. 512, shown here in 1955.

Members of Alexandria, Virginia, Troop No. 1 pose for their school yearbook in 1942. Troop No. 1 was sponsored by St. Agnes School and led by teacher Henricka Stebbins. Alexandria was the smallest of the five councils that merged in 1963 with only five percent of the total girl population of the new council. In contrast, Arlington brought 11 percent of the membership; National Capital, 39 percent; Northern Virginia, 23 percent; and Southern Maryland, 22 percent. Regardless, the merger committee voted to give each legacy council an equal vote in plans for the new organization. (Courtesy of St. Stephen's & St. Agnes School Archives, Alexandria, Virginia.)

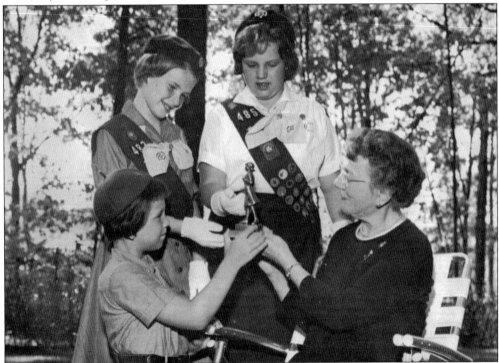

Mrs. Milton E. Hartley, right, shares the story of the Fairfax County Girl Scout Council. The council was organized in 1946 with 26 troops, 476 girls, and a budget of $5,825. By 1958, the council had grown to 485 troops, comprised of 7,800 girls and 2,700 adults. Hartley was president of the council from its creation until 1950.

The presidents of the five councils that merged to create Nation's Capital are presented with the US postage stamp commemorating the 50th birthday of Girl Scouting at the Woodward and Lothrop Coin and Stamp Department in 1962. From left to right are Bobby Lerch of National Capital, Adelaide Stegman of Arlington, Helen Gutman of Northern Virginia, Dot Davis of Alexandria, and Mary Walker of Southern Maryland.

World Chief Guide Lady Olave Baden-Powell visited Washington, DC, on March 11, 1962, to celebrate the 50th anniversary of Girl Scouts. The ambassadors of 51 countries joined local Girl Scouts at the Departmental Auditorium on Constitution Avenue NW. The complicated logistics involving all five local councils to arrange her visit convinced National Capital president Bobby Lerch that the merger could work.

WHAT'S YOUR CHOICE?

Those who are working on the organization of our new areawide council want to have your and your girls' opinions about what the council's name should be. Please register your choice below, and mail it to the office before July 1. Included on the ballot are some names that have already been suggested.

- - - - - - - - - CUT OUT HERE - - - - - - - - - -

My choice of name for our new council is:
( ) Potomac River Council
( ) Nation's Capital Council
( ) Greater Washington Council
( ) My suggestion_____
                    Name_____
                    Troop or District_____

As the regional merger process progressed, the National Capital Council invited members to vote on possible names for the new council and published a ballot in the June 1962 issue of *Trefoil*, the council newsletter. The ultimate winner was "Nation's Capital."

Leslie Schramm, chairman of Region III of the Girl Scouts of the USA, presents the charter establishing the Girl Scout Council of the Nation's Capital to E. Everett Ashley III, acting president, on January 8, 1963. Ashley chaired the intercouncil merger committee.

Representing the National Capital Girl Scout Council, Ethel Harvey played a key role in the negotiations that led to the creation of the Nation's Capital Council in 1963. In 1972, Harvey was elected president of Nation's Capital, becoming the first African American president of any Girl Scout council in the country. She held that post until 1978 and was credited with helping unify the diverse council. The President's Award in Honor of Ethel G. Harvey was created to recognize a girl member who has demonstrated outstanding leadership qualities.

As the number of African American troops grew, the District of Columbia Council split District VII into DC East and DC West, with South Capitol Street as the dividing line. Ethel Harvey chaired DC West, and Alma Jackson chaired DC East. Ernestine Lincoln, left, presented Jackson, right, with an award for her work.

Past and present Nation's Capital presidents reunited at the 2009 Annual Meeting. Pictured are, from left to right, (sitting) Susan K. Guthridge, Bobby Lerch, and Lynn Heebner; (standing) Kathy J. McKinless, Barbara Lowis Lehmann, Lois E. Bell, Diane Tipton, Donella Brockington, and Angela Lancaster.

Frederick Girl Scouts are seen with Frances Randall, publisher of the *Frederick Post* newspaper and Frederick's oldest Girl Scout, a member since 1938. In 2009, the Randall family and the newspaper provided the funds to renovate a unit now known as Randall Woods at Camp Potomac Woods.

Troops Nos. 85, 87, and 99 of Brunswick, Maryland, parade through town in the 1960s. Frederick County troops had been part of the Central Maryland and Penn Laurel Councils before joining Nation's Capital in 2006.

When Western Maryland Railroad donated Locomotive No. 817's bell to the Girl Scouts, Senior Wing Troop No. 20 dedicated the bell at Camp Misty Mount on June 19, 1955. The bell called Girl Scouts to meals at both Misty Mount and Camp CoHeLo until it vanished in 1974. It later resurfaced and was given to the Hagerstown Police Department, located in a former train station. However, the Washington County Girl Scout Alumnae Association began a campaign to put the bell on public display. Their wish was granted and on June 20, 2004, original members of Troop No. 20 helped dedicate the bell at its new home in Hagerstown City Park.

On May 9, 2009, the members of Shawnee Girl Scout Council voted to become part of the Girl Scout Council of the Nation's Capital. The signing ceremony included the original presidents of both councils. Pictured are, from left to right, (first row) Jan Verhage, executive director of Nation's Capital; Diane Tipton, president of Nation's Capital; Gertrude "Bobby" Lerch, president of Nation's Capital in 1963; Marguerite Cyr, president of Shawnee in 1963; Berniece Collis, president of Shawnee; and Maggie Witherbee, chief executive officer of Shawnee.

After the merger ceremony, the Girl Scouts from Shawnee held a bridging ceremony with the Nation's Capital Council president Diane Tipton, left, and outgoing Shawnee Council president Berniece Collis. Shawnee brought 5,000 members and 491 troops to the expanded council.

Four

Hiker, Rambler, Troop Camper

Camping is a fundamental part of the Girl Scout program. It teaches cooperation, self-reliance, respect for nature, and practical skills such as building fires and cooking. Most of all, camping is a shared experience that bonds girls together. Years later, girls and women still fondly remember campfire songs, the taste of burnt marshmallows, and whose tent collapsed in pouring rain.

The first Girl Scout troops in the Washington council were avid campers, but had no permanent camp of their own. Instead, they used public lands, such as Rock Creek Park, and borrowed land from other organizations or private owners.

Troop No. 1 created their own camp by leasing, repairing, and furnishing an abandoned four-room cabin in Bradley Hills (Bethesda) that they dubbed "Sunflower Lodge," as their patrol crest was the Sunflower.

Nation's Capital currently operates eight camp properties. The oldest is May Flather, which opened in 1930 in Mount Solon, Virginia. There are three other camps in Virginia, namely Coles Trip (Stafford County), Crowell (Fairfax County), and the largest camp, Potomac Woods (Loudoun County). In Maryland, Brighton Woods is in upper Montgomery County, Aquasco is in Prince George's County, and Winona is in Charles County. The "newest" camp is White Rock in West Virginia, which joined Nation's Capital along with Shawnee Council in 2009, but Girls Scouts have been camping there since the 1930s. The council also uses county parks, community centers, churches, and other public buildings for day camps in the summer and during school breaks.

Over the years, many camp properties have been bought, borrowed, or sold. The District of Columbia Council purchased Bay Breeze from the Boy Scouts in 1956 and operated the camp until 1974, when it was sold to the state of Maryland. The land is now part of Calvert Cliffs State Park. Camp Civitan in Olney, Maryland, was very popular for day and troop camping, as was Cosoma in St. Mary's County, Maryland. The Southern Maryland Council used Camp Moyane for many years; it was located across the Potomac River from the Mount Vernon estate. Alexandria Girl Scouts operated Camp Tapawingo, while the Arlington Council used Moss Ridge, a National Park Service camp, in the early 1940s before it established Potomac Woods. Finally, Plato Place in Forestville, Maryland, was run by "Uncle John" Plato, who created a nature preserve with three artificial lakes and invited local Girl Scouts and Campfire Girls to come and enjoy. A June 1974 land swap traded Plato Place for land that would be developed into Aquasco Farms.

The council offers six different types of camping for troops and individual girls. Sleep-away camps last one week, and groups of about six campers sleep in glen shelters or platform tents. About 3,500 girls attended a sleep-away camp in 2012. Day and evening camps offer activities during the day or evening, letting girls still get home for sports practice or other commitments. Community-based camps invite girls to sample Girl Scouting for a week and hopefully join a troop in the fall. Troops can head for the woods by renting a campsite and planning their own meals and activities. Many Girl Scout camps now have at least one heated lodge available for winter camping as well. Core camps provide meals and activities, giving novice troop leaders an introduction to camping—or veteran leaders a weekend to relax. Finally, since 2010, adult volunteers have had their own weekend at Camp White Rock. Camp Getaway lets leaders have their own turn on the archery range, ropes course, and pool with plenty of time to swap stories and program ideas.

Camping creates strong bonds that are celebrated for many years. The first season at May Flather ended in August 1930, and the first Camp May Flather reunion was held in December 1930. By the December 31, 1931, reunion, the event was already designated an "annual event" and drew 300 Girl Scouts and guests to an evening of song, stories, and a movie about the camp. May Flather hosted a 50th Anniversary Weekend Extravaganza in October 1980, a 63rd reunion in 1993, and a 75th anniversary celebration in July 2005 that included one camper from the 1930 season.

The Share Her Annual Real Expense (SHARE) annual giving campaign provides financial assistance for girls who need help paying for camp, while fall sales of magazines, nuts, and candy go toward camp maintenance. The Jan Verhage Endowment for Camperships was established in 2010 when Nation's Capital executive director Jan Verhage left Washington to become chief operating officer of GSUSA in New York City. The Endowment ensures that the fun and rewards of a Girl Scout summer sleep-away camp experience are available to every girl, regardless of her family's financial situation.

Washington's first Girl Scouts used the outer edges of the District of Columbia as their camp. In 1923, Troop No. 10 took the trolley out to the district line near Cabin John, Maryland, to begin a day hike to the Chain Bridge over the Potomac River. The trolley tracks can be seen in the snow behind them.

The first "official" camp uniform was introduced in 1925 and consisted of a white middy blouse and black bloomers. The stylish ensemble inspired the following popular camp song: "Middies, bloomers, middies, bloomers all day long; She wears them in the morning, she wears them at noon; She only takes them off by the light of the moon, Wooo!"

The first District of Columbia Girl Scout camp was Camp Bradley, at Edgewood Arsenal (now Aberdeen Proving Ground) in Magnolia, Maryland, in 1921. Thanks to the help of Gen. Amos O. Fries, Camp Bradley had boardwalks, electricity, and running water, while the nearby Boy Scout camp had to make do with kerosene lamps and a pump. The Army invited the girls to try tear gas one day. After much discomfort, they declared the experience to be one of the best of the camp session.

Each unit at Camp Bradley, in Aberdeen, Maryland, was responsible for cooking its own food. Breakfast usually meant fruit, cereal, or eggs and bacon, plus hot muffins or biscuits, washed down with plenty of fresh milk. Dinner, at least on Sundays, meant roast beef, potatoes with gravy, beans, and cake. Suppers usually offered sandwiches and soup, applesauce, cookies, more milk—and ice cream!

The US government loaned Fort Foote for summer camp in 1927, and it was used for weekend camping trips well into the 1930s. Located near Fort Washington, Maryland, the fort sits on a bluff high above the Potomac River. Campers, like (from left to right) Lois Hall, Eileen Magruder, Betty Brundage, Margaret Cooke, and Virginia Reading of Troop No. 12, were told to bring four middy blouses (white for dress and khaki), two pairs of bloomers (black for dress), and underwear "plain and strong." The District of Columbia Council tried to purchase Fort Foote in December 1927. Troops demonstrated their various Girl Scout skills in department store windows in downtown Washington, while their leaders stood outside on the sidewalks with collection cans.

Staff posed for the camera at Camp Matoaka, located in St. Leonards, Maryland, on the Chesapeake Bay. Mrs. James Alburtus loaned the camp to the Girl Scouts from August 24 to September 17, 1928. Girls paid $9 per week plus $3 for round-trip bus transportation.

These campers at Camp Matoaka seem less excited than their counselors in this photograph. Notice that they are, however, all properly dressed for a day of exploring at camp; they are wearing their middy blouses, bloomers, brimmed hats, and very sturdy shoes.

First Lady Lou Henry Hoover attended the dedication of Camp May Flather in Virginia, spending the night of August 7–8, 1930, in a tent. She formally unveiled the new Hoover Bridge by cutting an ivy rope draped across the rails and walking across. The 100-foot span was her personal gift as the honorary national president of Girl Scouts.

By the time campers arrive, the staff has already trained together for several weeks. Senior staff members have college degrees and extensive experience working with girls. Pictured here, the staff selected for Camp May Flather's second season in 1931 had degrees from Ohio State, Columbia, the New York State College of Forestry, and Harrisonburg State Teachers College.

For over 50 years, members of the Mitchell family have been caretakers for Camp May Flather, starting with Bill Mitchell. "Uncle Billy" was there when the camp first opened in 1930 and taught basket weaving classes in addition to his caretaker duties.

The Boone Unit from Camp May Flather meets a family from one of the neighboring farms in the 1930s. The camp's first director, Dorothy Greene, worked hard to cultivate the good will of the camp's neighbors, using their skills, labor, and building supplies.

The staff at Camp White Rock in West Virginia posed for a photograph around 1938. For years, Alison Cooper, an active Girl Scout in Winchester, Virginia, and her husband, Eugene B. Cooper, rented their campground to the Girl Scouts and Boy Scouts (on separate weeks, of course). The Winchester Girl Scout council purchased the property in 1952, and it became the flagship Girl Scout camp in the Shenandoah Mountains.

During the Depression, the Works Progress Administration built an outhouse at Camp White Rock. It took four men one week to dig the pit and construct the building. Next, they painted the facility a silver color inside and out and tacked instructions to the door. First Lady Eleanor Roosevelt signed the instructions, so the latrine has been known ever since as "the Eleanor Roosevelt."

The District of Columbia Council purchased Camp Brighton Woods in 1958. The 60-acre camp in Montgomery County, Maryland, offers plenty of opportunities to hike, study nature, craft, and practice archery. It is used for both day and troop camping.

This is the ribbon-cutting ceremony for the 6,400-square-foot lodge at Brighton Woods in 1991. From left to right are Girl Scout Junior Alcadia Tambunga, council past president Barbara Lowis Lehmann, assistant executive director Tammy Woodbury, Nation's Capital president Lois Bell, longtime volunteer Mary Wood, and Girl Scout Junior Mary Ann Lawson. Two new lodges, Friendship and Meadowside, were dedicated on October 24, 2010. Building funds were donated by Montgomery County, the State of Maryland, Clark Construction, and Lockheed Martin.

Brownies pictured here work together to stir up a pot of stone soup at Brighton Woods. Stone soup is a favorite one-pot meal: every girl brings one ingredient and they are all combined into one pot for dinner. Girls learn to make progressively more complicated recipes both indoors and out.

Campers get up close to nature with a new frog friend at Camp Crowell in Fairfax County, Virginia, in 1961. The Fairfax County Girl Scout Council acquired the land from Mr. and Mrs. Thomas J. Crowell in 1948, and it opened for camping in 1950. Additional buildings have been added over the years, including the Vickie Hurst cook shelter, dedicated to a longtime volunteer. Crowell is the only Nation's Capital camp with a tree house unit.

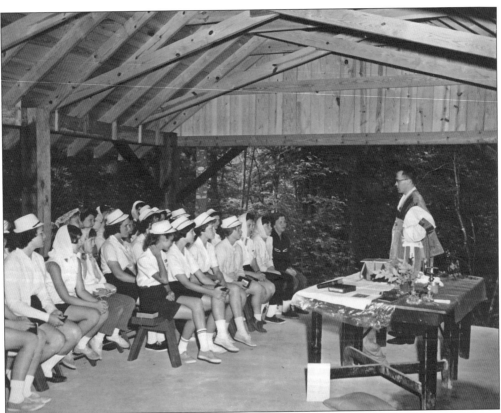

HYATTSVILLE, MD., *July 12* 1938

Ninety — days after date for value received, I, we jointly and severally promise to pay to the order of *The Prince Georges Bank & Trust Co*

Fifteen hundred Dollars

with interest until paid at 5%

at the **PRINCE GEORGES BANK & TRUST COMPANY**

In consideration whereof the makers and endorsers hereon jointly and severally do waive all notice, demand and protest and in default of payment of this note they do further authorize any Justice of the Peace or Clerk of any Court of record, in Maryland or elsewhere, to enter judgment hereon by confession before, at or after maturity against us for the amount hereof, interest and costs, including an attorney's fee of ten per cent., expressly waiving summons or other process, and do further consent to immediate execution of said judgment, expressly waiving the benefit of all exemption laws.

WITNESS *Regina S. Bexley, Sec.*

Address

NO. *3285*

18 75

$1500 00

1518 75

DUE *Oct. 10, 1938*

Camp Conestoga opened in 1939 off Good Luck Road near Greenbelt in Prince George's County, Maryland. Prince George's County Council officers took out a $1,518.75 loan to build a cabin on the 50-acre site. After trespassers burned the camp's log cabin to the ground in 1961, a prefabricated steel cabin was erected in 1962.

The Prince George's County Council purchased land in Hughesville, Maryland, in 1955 to create a 178-acre resident camp. Several names were proposed for the new camp, including Stony Hill, Catch as Catch Can, and Jennifer Farm, before settling on Winona, a Native American name meaning "first-born daughter." The camp held an international-themed "Little Roundup" in June 1961 for teens, during which the first Catholic Mass was celebrated at the camp.

Camp Winona, still known as the "Hughesville Camp," was dedicated on September 16, 1956. Troop No. 9 was the first to camp there. Winona was renovated in 2008 and now has flush toilets, five lodges, and six glen shelter units. The camp can accommodate up to 319 campers.

Meteorologist Susan Ducey (back row, left) led the weather watchers' unit at Camp Tuckerman in 1991. The first weather badge was introduced in 1947. The day camp has operated continuously since 1986 but has existed since the 1960s.

Both the Girl Scouts of Frederick County, Maryland, and the Prince George's County/Southern Maryland Council used Misty Mount as a residential camp. Located in the Catoctin Mountains, the camp offered plenty of opportunities for hiking and creeking.

Misty Mount also had a swimming pool and offered classes in "swimming ballet," according to the camp brochures.

Camp Aquasco in Prince George's County offers 172 acres divided into two sections. One half of the camp is undeveloped and perfect for primitive camping, while the other half has a lodge and glen shelters. The land is leased from the Maryland–National Capital Park and Planning Commission. Much of the land improvement has been done by teen Girl Scouts.

No camping trip is complete without at least one s'more, the tasty toasted-marshmallow, graham cracker, and chocolate bar treat. The recipe was first published in the 1927 book *Tramping and Trailing with the Girl Scouts*. Many variations exist, including substituting the colorful Peeps candy for regular marshmallows.

Camp starts at the bus depot, where volunteers tag and stow luggage, assign girls to buses, and start singing camp songs. In the 1920s and 1930s, the bus left from the Little House on New York Avenue NW and cost $1–3. Now campers depart from the Fairfax County Government Center in Virginia or Cresthaven Elementary School in Silver Spring, Maryland, and a round-trip ticket is $40.

Next, it is time to meet the camp director and be sorted into units. There always are a few girls who are dropped off at camp, so it is time to greet them now. Campers also finally will meet their own counselors, but they will not learn their real name. Tradition dictates that all staff be addressed only by their camp names. Carefully chosen to reflect their personalities, camp names may be based on nature, sports, food, or popular culture.

Camp May Flather used an innovative layout that resembled a small village. Instead of central barracks, girls were divided into five independent units, each with about six glen shelters, a washroom, and field kitchen. This unit, from 1931, housed four girls in each glen shelter. Recreation specialists from around the world visited May Flather to see this new approach firsthand.

Older campers, like the teens who participated in the 1961 Little Roundup at Camp Winona, often bunk in platform tents. Each morning, campers roll up the flaps to let fresh air in.

Many resident camps include one "wilderness overnight," where girls sleep under the stars and cook dinner using food carried in their backpacks. May Flather and Potomac Woods have both offered horseback programs that included an overnight ride.

In 1949, a flash flood dumped four inches of rain at Camp May Flather as counselors were arriving to set up camp. From left to right, Faith Marr, Kay Ducharme, Eugenia D., and Grace McDade, along with camp director Edith Clark (not shown) were marooned for 48 hours before they were rescued. Note the damage to the road.

Dishwashing at camp requires three buckets or tubs. The first tub holds hot, soapy water. The second tub holds clean water for rinsing. The third tub has either boiling water or cool water and a sanitizing solution. Once dishes have been placed in all three tubs, they are hung in net bags to dry.

Meals at a resident camp, such as Potomac Woods, are served family style. Each unit sits together at the same table, and two girls at a time take turns as the "hopper," serving the others.

Nature study is part of every camp. At Holland Acres day camp, in Centreville, Virginia, in June 1962, fourth graders made leaf blue prints. Day camps usually have a theme, which may be related to nature or not. Camp Crowell in Oakton, Virginia, is used for troop camping and is home to Camp Crossroads, a Harry Potter–themed day camp, and Ashgrove Adventure, which had an African Safari theme for 2013.

The fifth and sixth graders at Holland Acres were assigned to the Survival Unit, where they made a lashed shelter with tree boughs. Holland Acres was sold in 1973, and the area is now a subdivision.

Plato Place in Forestville, Maryland, featured three artificial lakes and canoe races. "Uncle John" Plato also built a toboggan run covered with piles of fall leaves. These campers from 1962 are getting ready for their next downhill adventure.

Many resident camps have winterized cabins, but a February 1958 snowstorm left Arlington Troop No. 163 snowbound at Potomac Woods in Loudoun County, Virginia. With local roads impassable, an Army helicopter picked up the 18 girls and their two leaders and flew them to Fort Belvoir. A local farmer cleared a path from the camp to a field where the helicopter landed.

The Potomac Woods RiverWalk teaches girls and adults the importance of managing natural resources and preserving them for future generations. The RiverWalk, which has its own patch, was dedicated on Mother's Day in 2009, which is appropriate, since it was a generous gift from Sarah Phillips, right, and her daughter Barbara Sutton, left, both longtime Girl Scouts from Loudoun County, Virginia.

Over the years, hundreds of campers have squeezed into the Potomac Woods Pooh Tree, a stately 80-foot-tall sycamore tree on the banks of the Potomac River. It looks like at least seven girls are in there with council president Diane Tipton.

The Fairfax County Girl Scout Council purchased the land for Camp Coles Trip in December 1954. County records had a map of the area labeled "Coal Strip." Located in Stafford County, Virginia, Coles Trip offers an aquatics program and prime hunting ground for fossils. Campers can earn the Coles Trip Treasures patch, which focuses on the ecosystem of Coles Trip and the Chesapeake Bay Watershed. Introduced in 2006, the patch program builds on other environmental education programs, such as the Water Drop patch program, developed with the Environmental Protection Agency and the Roots and Shoots badge program, created with the Jane Goodall Institute.

Long before cell phones and Global Positioning Systems, campers learned orienteering with a compass. Most Nation's Capital resident camps now have Geocaching courses that send girls to every corner of the camp.

For 2011, Camp Sunshine's theme was "Mystery in the Woods." The Cadette unit learned "low-tech" crime scene investigation techniques and compared different recipes for making "movie blood."

Over 500 Girl Scout Seniors attended a weekend encampment at Bull Run State Park in Manassas, Virginia, in 1969. High school–age troops tend to be small, so many troops participate in countywide groups that sponsor special events, travel opportunities, and other programs. Groups include TOGA (Taskforce for Older Girl Scouts of Ashgrove) in Virginia, MCOGL (Montgomery County Older Girls and Leaders) in Maryland, and FROG (Frederick Older Girls) for Frederick County, Maryland.

Weekend core camps are a great way to get acquainted with the great outdoors. A teen troop or a team of adults provides basic camp services—meals, program activities, campfires—so younger troops can get a taste of camping. Teen troops often run core camps to raise funds for an international trip.

The Rockwood National Program Center was located at 1101 MacArthur Boulevard in Potomac, Maryland, about 15 miles northwest of the US Capitol. Socialite Carolyn G. Caughey bequeathed the 93-acre property to the Girl Scouts in 1936. Caughey's gift was inspired by Helen Hopkins Zelov's bravery. Zelov was a Girl Scout leader who helped rescuers locate and save 11 victims when Washington's Knickerbocker Theatre collapsed from heavy snowfall on January 28, 1922. Seriously injured herself, Zelov was presented with a medal for bravery.

Girl Scouts from the District of Columbia–Montgomery County Council first camped at Rockwood in 1937. The council began renovations and built Adirondack shelters, but work stopped due to supply shortages during World War II. GSUSA then assumed responsibility for the estate, built troop houses, and renovated the Manor House in 1950–1952, dedicating rooms to Henrietta Bates Brooke and Lou Henry Hoover. The facility was officially dedicated as Rockwood National Girl Scout Camp in 1952. It was designated a National Program Center in 1964 and was renamed Rockwood Girl Scout National Center in 1971. (Courtesy of Mark Bowles.)

Lucy Knox, left, registers visitors arriving at Rockwood in 1960. As a national facility, Rockwood was open to African American troops before many local camps. Local troops helped with the upkeep at Rockwood, coming out on weekends to work on the gardens and help improve the trails.

Rockwood was very popular, as troops from all across the country—and even across the world—used it as their base camp when they visited Washington, DC. Local troops used it for a variety of events, and it served as a national and local training center. By 1978, some 20,000 girls visited Rockwood each year. Lady Baden-Powell (center), head of the Girl Guides, made several visits and enjoyed meeting the girls staying at Rockwood.

In April 1978, GSUSA announced it would sell Rockwood to a residential developer for $4.1 million. The organization explained the decision as one of cost cutting, noting that the older Macy National Center in New York provided similar services. Opposed to the move, Friends of Rockwood, a group of nine Girl Scouts and leaders, filed a class action lawsuit in Montgomery County, Maryland, arguing that the sale violated the terms of Caughey's will, which stipulated that should the Girl Scouts "abandon" the property or cease to use it for a "character building" purpose, it would revert to the Esther Chapter of the Order of the Eastern Star. Friends of Rockwood included, from left to right, (first row) Jean Moore, Jo Reynolds, and Jan Malone; (second row) Anna Foultz, Pauline Gearhart, and Anne Pomykala.

In May 1979, the Rescue Rockwood group marched in front of the White House, to attract the attention of First Lady Rosalyn Carter, honorary GSUSA president. The lawsuit was settled in 1981, when the developer agreed to set aside 20 acres, including the Manor House and other buildings, for the Maryland–National Capital Park and Planning Commission. Today, Rockwood is a popular venue for weddings and other events. Girl Scouts can camp overnight in the dormitories, but there are no cooking facilities available to them.

Five

MAKE THE WORLD A BETTER PLACE

Girl Scouting encourages girls to reach out to their communities, to realize that they are part of a larger entity, and to realize that they can make a difference. Girl Scouts work to make the world a better place through service projects and by treating all people equally.

The organization emerged as World War I began, and Girl Scouts quickly gained notice and praise for their wartime service. In December 1914, for example, Troop No. 5 of Takoma Park reported that its members were knitting scarves for European soldiers. After the United States entered the war, Girl Scouts made sandwiches and cakes for troops passing through Washington in 1917, often accompanying Lou Henry Hoover to local canteens. They continued the practice during the subsequent influenza epidemic, serving bowls of hot soup to children at Washington-area playgrounds. Herbert Hoover, then head of the Food Administration, wrote Juliette Gordon Low to praise the relief efforts, saying that he hoped other Girl Scouts "will follow the splendid example set by these girls in our Capital City."

During the Great Depression and World War II, Girl Scouts sold war bonds, collected scrap metal, and helped with meals, housework, and child care as their mothers took jobs. Leaders touted the benefits of camping as a way to learn self-sufficiency and how to keep entertained at very little cost.

Over the years, Girl Scouts have carried out thousands of service projects, such as food drives, visiting nursing homes, and assembling first aid kits. In 1921, the District of Columbia superintendent of parks asked for their help in keeping city parks clean. They have decorated veterans' graves at Arlington National Cemetery and served as "sidewalk babysitters," entertaining young children outside polling places while their mothers went inside to vote.

Service continued at camp as well. In the late 1930s and early 1940s, girls and staff at Camp May Flather carried out "blister rust control work," for the US Department of Agriculture. They identified affected white pine tress and pulled up gooseberry and other bushes affected by the disease.

The Girl Scouts of the Washington, DC, region also confronted the difficult issue of racial segregation. In the 1950s, councils began to quietly integrate summer camps. No grand public announcements were made regarding the shift. Instead, council staff went to the camp bus depots armed with checkbooks, ready to give refunds to families uncomfortable with integration. Few refunds were needed. By 1966, the summer camp brochure featured a cover photograph with both a white and an African American girl.

In March 1968, the National Advisory Commission on Civil Disorder released a landmark study warning that "our nation is moving toward two societies, one black, one white—separate and unequal." Known as the Kerner Report, as Illinois governor Otto Kerner chaired the panel, the report called for investment in housing and jobs to improve living conditions for African Americans and an end to segregation in urban neighborhoods, among other recommendations.

Pres. Lyndon B. Johnson rejected the Kerner Report's advice, but the Girl Scouts paid attention. At the 1969 National Council Session, GSUSA launched "Action 70," a program to improve race relations within Girl Scouting. GSUSA also held a conference in Atlanta in March 1970 to discuss ways to make Girl Scouting more relevant and responsive to African American girls. Dorothy Ferebee, a Washington physician who became the first African American vice president of GSUSA in 1969, chaired the conference and presented its results in a speech at the Nation's Capital's annual meeting in April 1970.

Within Nation's Capital, the leaders of the Southwest Montgomery County and Mid-Eastern Washington Associations took up the challenge of fostering good relationships within the council. Mary Ann Claxton of Southwest Montgomery County invited field vice president Ethel Harvey to a discussion on "the Kerner Report and Its Implications for Girl Scouting."

Harvey's discussion evolved into the Inter-Association Friendship Committee, a series of joint events between the Girl Scouts from the urban Mid-Eastern Washington and upper-middle class Southwest Montgomery County Associations spanning more than three decades. Led by Mary Rose Chappelle and Cathryn Finch, respectively, the Friendship Committee brought together troops for camping, swapping program ideas, service projects, and fun.

Hosting the National Council Session in Washington, DC, in 1975 also helped consolidate the Nation's Capital council. Harvey recalled the intense preparations:

> We invited people from all over the council—we invited people to participate that hadn't been involved before. And people that hadn't known each other and had never worked together came together and created an outstanding event. . . . And in the process, the Girl Scouts showed this whole region just how well all people could work together. I think this very important advance in race relations, and our council's efforts to play a role in improving society, is one of the things that people need to know about Girl Scouting.

Nation's Capital also looked inward, examining its policies and practices for unequal treatment. The council adopted an affirmative action plan for staff in 1974 and for volunteers in 1978, considerably earlier than the national organization.

During both World Wars, Girl Scouts planted Victory Gardens in many communities. In the Washington area, there were Victory Gardens at the Daughters of the American Revolution headquarters, at Thirteenth and Iowa Avenue NW, and here at First and T Street NE. (Harris and Ewing Collection, Library of Congress.)

Even Brownies did their part in the war effort. These young ladies from College Park, Maryland, went door-to-door in their neighborhoods in 1945, filling wagons, boxes, and barrels with scrap metal.

In 1944, Troop No. 42 of Takoma Park, Maryland, spent Saturdays selling stamps and bonds to people at the Woolworth on Laurel Street. They alternated weekends with Troop No. 36 and sang songs to attract the attention of passing shoppers.

Girl Scouts quickly gained a reputation as a wholesome, reliable, and well-mannered group of young women. As a result, civic groups often would request a troop to work at an event. Mystery writer Mary Roberts Rinehart, in the light-colored dress, asked for a Girl Scout "honor guard" when she gave a large tea at her home on Massachusetts Avenue on November 12, 1924. One of the girls present, Phyllis Adelman, recalled, "Being a member of a fully uniformed troop when scouting was only ten years old was a privilege because we were often asked to assist at social functions in Washington . . . The uniforms were made of heavy khaki cotton and the pork pie hats must have been very unflattering, but we felt proud to wear them." (Harris and Ewing Collection, Library of Congress.)

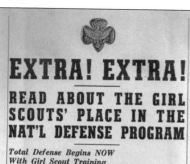

EXTRA! EXTRA!

READ ABOUT THE GIRL SCOUTS' PLACE IN THE NAT'L DEFENSE PROGRAM

Total Defense Begins NOW With Girl Scout Training

HEALTH AND SAFETY TRAINING. Proper nutrition and good health habits are fundamentals in maintaining physical fitness, and play a major role in the Girl Scout program.

TRAINING FOR CITIZENSHIP is a vital part of defense and preparedness program. Experiences in democratic living make basic contribution to strength of country.

TRAINING FOR EFFECTIVE SERVICE. Girls want to share in preparedness program. Girls DO share by giving hundreds of hours of their time and skill. They release adults for more important defense work.

TRAINING FOR CONSERVATION AND THRIFT. Girl Scouts cook, shop, plan meals, garden, and preserve fruits and vegetables. They sew, mend, and make useful articles.

MAINTENANCE OF NORMAL INTERESTS. Regardless of emergency, girls are still girls and they must continue to lead balanced lives. They enjoy hobbies and pet interests, and have a host of recreational resources up their sleeves.

Girl Scouts Need Leaders

1500 GIRLS IN OUR COMMUNITY WANT to become Girl Scouts, but are deprived of this privilege because of lack of volunteer leaders.

HERE IS AN OPPORTUNITY FOR YOU — to give community service and make your contribution to the National Defense Program by helping girls to help themselves.

Call Your Local Headquarters

WASHINGTON GIRL SCOUTS
1825 M Street, N. W.   NAtional 0400

Girl Scouts endeavored to play a useful role in national defense during World War II. First aid, sewing, cooking, child care, and other skills were learned and put to good use by the many women who left home and entered the workforce.

Arlington's Troop No. 41 practiced a scenario where they transported victims from the rubble of a "bombed" apartment building. The Girl Scout Council is hopeful that they never actually have to put that skill to use in their everyday lives.

Sewing and other needlework badges have been available since the first handbook was published in 1913. Many girls made their own uniforms, and the first troops embroidered their own badges. The girls of Arlington Junior Troop No. 146 are sewing aprons and other projects for the home.

Members of Junior Troops Nos. 434 and 472 of Prince George's County put their sewing skills to work for others, sewing and stuffing dolls that will be Christmas gifts for students at the Rosewood State Training School for the Mentally Retarded.

As the driving force behind the Inter-Association Friendship Committee, Mary Rose Chappelle, left, and Cathryn Finch helped unite a diverse council. They also developed a close friendship that lasted more than 30 years. (Courtesy Mary Rose Chappelle.)

The Inter-Association Friendship Committee sponsored many events over the years, but one of the most popular was Brownie Pretzel Day, shown here on November 21, 1992. Hundreds of Brownies made thousands of pretzels over the years. (Courtesy Mary Rose Chappelle.)

Since 1986, the Inter-Association Friendship Committee has sponsored a joint workday with troops from Washington, DC, and lower Montgomery County, Maryland. The girls gather at Glen Echo Park to polish the brass on the historic carousel before the park opens to the public for the season.

From left to right, Mary Rose Chappelle, Marva Johnson, Mae Barnes, Beulah Sutherland, Ethel Harvey, and Therese Grossman arrive at the "United Under the Green" celebration on March 10, 1995. The evening, held at Central High School in Capital Heights, Maryland, honored African American women who have made outstanding contributions to the Girl Scout Council of the Nation's Capital.

Nation's Capital ran a day camp at Carver Terrace, a public housing complex in Northwest Washington, DC, in 1995. Each year, hundreds of non–Girl Scouts participate in community outreach camps for under-served communities. They enjoy games, field trips, and a chance to just be kids.

Teen Troop No. 2890 of Montgomery Village, Maryland, collected 175 new and gently used bras for victims of domestic violence as part of the 2012 Soma Intimates campaign. In 1999, Shawnee Council highlighted the issue of domestic violence by creating the "Stop Domestic Violence" patch program.

Troops from across the council have participated in the "Girl Scouts Forever Green" initiative. The program encourages girl-led projects that promote simple steps toward greener living, such as changing to energy efficient compact fluorescent lightbulbs. Pepco helped purchase 5,000 CFL bulbs for low-income homes. Over 14,000 bulbs were changed through this program.

Bethesda Girl Scout Troop No. 6002 joined with Chesapeake Natives Inc., an area nonprofit, to provide locally native plants for Montgomery County's Locust Grove Nature Center on Democracy Boulevard.

Girl Scouts presented flowers and Mother's Day cards to women whose sons served in the Vietnam War. The girls arranged over 500 cards from Washington-area elementary schools along the Vietnam Veteran's Memorial on May 13, 2001. The event recognized an often forgotten group of women and helped the girls connect with this era of US history.

Girl Scouts have helped decorate the graves at Arlington National Cemetery since the 1920s. Cadette Troop No. 1592 of Germantown, Maryland, laid wreaths on the headstones on December 15, 2011, as part of Wreaths Across America day.

Springfield, Virginia's, Cadette Troop No. 282 worked at a food drive at Lorton Community Action Center (LCAC). The teens were put in charge of loading the collected food into a LCAC truck, following it to a food bank, and unloading the donations. The day of service was topped off with dinner and a movie.

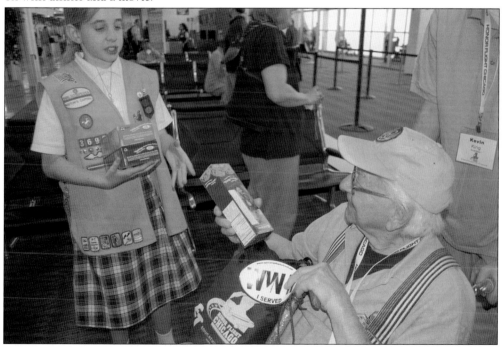

Members of Cadette Troop No. 3690 greeted World War II veterans as their June 23, 2010, Honor Flight arrived at Dulles airport. Girl Scouts escorted the veterans to their waiting bus so they could visit the National World War II Memorial in Washington, DC. Girls handed out boxes of Girl Scout cookies for the veterans to munch on, including the appropriately named "Thank U Berry Munch."

Troop No. 112 from Landover, Maryland, participated in the Red Cross Holiday Mail for Heroes program in November 2012. They made Christmas and holiday cards for US troops fighting overseas because they appreciate all that these brave men and women do.

Food drives are a staple of Girl Scout service projects. Many events, such as movie night or cosmic bowling, ask for a canned good as the price of admission. Sometimes entire weekends are devoted to a super-sized food drive. Members of Brownie Troop No. 2777 in Silver Spring, Maryland, helped collect nonperishable food items at the Aspen Hill Giant grocery store for the Manna Food Service/Help Feed the Hungry Food Drive. A total of 32,260 pounds of food was collected from the participating Giant stores.

Six

SOMETHING FOR
ALL THE GIRLS

From camping to cooking, horses to history, and maps to mysteries, Girl Scouting has something for everyone. The core Girl Scout program—badges, Journeys, Gold Award, and so on—comes from the national organization, but each council develops unique programs based on local interests, resources, and opportunities.

The Nation's Capital Council naturally offers a range of programs related to citizenship and patriotism. Teens can work at a presidential inauguration, spend a week as a Congressional Aide, visit their state legislature, or hone their advocacy skills by earning the African Americans in Congress patch. In 2010, 18 Senior and Ambassador Girl Scouts visited Capitol Hill to encourage passage of the Healthy Media for Youth Act after studying how the media depicts women and girls.

Recognizing that girls often reject courses and careers in science, technology, engineering, and mathematics (STEM), Girl Scouts has committed to providing fun, real-world activities to get girls into science. The "Make the Connection" program, sponsored by Booz Allen Hamilton, introduces girls to the range of careers in these fields. Nation's Capital also partners with the Smithsonian National Air and Space Museum for an annual Girl Scout Day. Events have been held at both the main museum on the National Mall and at the Udvar-Hazy Center in Chantilly, Virginia. Five Girl Scout teens brainstormed new computer apps at the first White House "Codeathon" in December 2012.

The annual cookie program teaches girls about budgeting, marketing, and goal setting, but cookies are only part of the financial literacy program. Before the national program portfolio introduced financial literacy badges for each age level in 2011, Nation's Capital had created its own badge program, Capital Currency. Grants from Capital One bank helped develop Capital Currency, and company employees helped run weekend workshops for girls earning the badges. Capital One continues to support financial literacy by funding the Financial Fitness Challenge.

Museums and theaters in the greater Washington area frequently provide special programs for Girl Scouts, including discounted tickets, special behind-the-scenes tours, and even sleepovers. Troops can meet Martha Washington at the Mount Vernon estate in Virginia, make their own Fabergé egg at Hillwood Estate, hike the C&O Canal, and learn the secrets of espionage at the International Spy Museum. Girls experience 18th-century travel options when they spend the night at Gadsby's Tavern Museum in Alexandria, Virginia, see what sharks do at midnight at the National Aquarium, or experience colonial life at Dumbarton House in Washington. Thousands of girls have attended special Girl Scout–only performances of the Nutcracker by the Washington Ballet, where dancers answer girls' questions after the show. Girls become the stars of the show themselves with the DC Step Showcase at Trinity College in Washington, DC. Introduced in 2007, the annual competition has developed into one of the council's most popular events.

Girl Scouting strives to provide programs and opportunities for all girls, irrespective of race, religion, economic level, or physical and cognitive abilities. Troops for girls with hearing and vision disabilities have been created, and these girls have also been included in mixed troops as well. In 1983, Nation's Capital introduced a Hearing Awareness patch developed with the Suzanne Pathy Speak Up Institute. The program taught girls the challenges faced by the hearing impaired and ways to protect their own hearing. The Southern Maryland Council established Troop No. 947 at the Gallatin Street Center for children with intellectual disabilities in College Park, Maryland, in 1957.

Nation's Capital has an inclusion specialist on staff, as well as linguistic outreach specialists, to help reach families that may not be fluent in English. All age levels can earn the Including All Girls patch, which increases awareness, understanding, and acceptance of people's differences and disabilities. In 1993, Christine Hoehl became the nation's first Girl Scout with Down syndrome to earn the Gold Award.

Girls have sampled other cultures, religions, and traditions by earning the Hispanic Heritage, Common Threads, and Open Houses of Faith patches.

Conflict resolution skills are encouraged and developed in the Increase the Peace and Zoo Animal Safari patch programs.

Non–Girl Scouts also have opportunities to develop their skills and sample Girl Scout traditions. Day camps like Camp Butterfly and Camp Chica or evening programs like Camp Lightning Bug are offered during school breaks and summer vacations. The annual Encuentro de Chicas Latinas (Convening of Latina Youth Leaders) offers leadership empowerment, career mentoring, and guest speakers, blended with dancing, high adventure sports, and fun. Howard University also hosts 200 girls for the annual "Your Turn to Lead" program, which encourages activism in schools and communities.

Parachute games promote cooperation and coordination. Brownie Sports and Games Day, held April 6, 1991, at Bethesda United Methodist Church, offered activities to earn the Brownie Sports and Games Try-It. (Courtesy Mary Rose Chappelle.)

Nation's Capital held the first STEM Leadership Institute on April 20, 2013. Exclusively for Cadettes, participants explored science, technology, engineering, and math, and the leadership institute gave them an inside look at the University of Maryland at College Park campus. After completing the institute, the Cadettes can earn their Leader in Action award by helping a Brownie troop complete a Journey.

In 1988, 1989, and 1990, Shawnee Council sponsored Pedal Pushers, a Wider Opportunity (now known as Destinations). Each year, approximately 40 teen girls from across the United States bicycled 185 miles along the C&O Canal between Cumberland, Maryland, and Washington, DC. The girls visited sites like McMahon's Mill in Williamsport, Maryland, and camped along the way.

Girl Scouts learn the value of teamwork, develop their problem-solving skills, and build confidence on the challenge course. Camp May Flather, Crowell, and White Rock all have high-adventure facilities. Girls can experience the ropes courses, climbing walls, and zip lines.

Teen Girl Scouts can learn more about their state government by attending the annual "Legislative Days." The program began in Richmond, Virginia, in 1983 and expanded to Maryland in 1984 and the District of Columbia in 1985. Nation's Capital Council staff work with the local school systems so that participants, such as these girls visiting the Maryland State legislature in Annapolis in 1992, are excused from school for the day.

Nation's Capital president Barbara Lowis Lehmann launched the Congressional Aide program in 1975. Girls selected for the program spend one week during the summer shadowing a Congressional staff member. Congressional Aides greet visitors, give tours, attend hearings, and assist with research. Girl Scouts come away from the program with a better understanding of how governments work and how to pursue a career in public service. The 2010 Congressional Aides met former House Speaker Nancy Pelosi (center).

The Montgomery County Older Girls and Leaders (MCOGL) group sponsored Caves to Comets, a high-adventure camp at Brighton Woods in 1998. Included as a part of this event was a trip to Lincoln Caverns in Pennsylvania. (Courtesy Graydon Moss.)

Brownie Troop No. 1273 celebrated the end of the 2010–2011 school year with camping at the Tree House Camp and rafting at Harpers Ferry, West Virginia. These paddlers have their gear in hand and are ready and raring to go as soon as their leader lets them off the bus!

During World War II, Girl Scouts were encouraged to make the best of wartime shortages. The Little House in Washington offered a workshop in October 1942 with many ingenious tips, such as making a chair from an orange crate and wastebaskets from coffee cans. These Senior Scouts from Frederick, Maryland, also learned how to plan meals around food rationing.

Senior Troop No. 14 of Cheverly, Maryland, led a canned food drive in April 1946. Wearing the typical wartime uniform are, from left to right, Helen Winks, Anne Louise Scheidt, Evelyn Smith, Winnie McKenzie, Audrey Owens, Sarah Humphries, and Bunky Myers.

The DC Step Showcase debuted in 2007 and has become one of the council's most popular events. Nine teams competed before a crowd of 1,500 for the 2013 title. Council CEO Lidia Soto-Harmon congratulated the Mountaineer Steppers of Troops Nos. 40480, 40726, and 40939 for their winning "Rosie the Riveter" routine.

Junior Troop No. 1988 listens closely as NASA astrophysicist Carol Jo Crannell explains her sun project in the clean room at the Goddard Space Flight Center in Greenbelt, Maryland, in 1999.

In October 1975, GSCNC launched the Riley's Lockhouse History Program through a special permit from the C&O Canal National Historical Park. Bethesda, Maryland, Cadette Troop No. 2032, searching for a special way to mark the US bicentennial, devised a project to demonstrate how lockhouse families lived in the 1870s. Over 30 years later, Girl Scout troops still change into costumes and give tours on Saturdays and Sundays in the spring and fall.

Girls demonstrate daily chores from the 1870s, including washing clothes, making butter, singing, playing games, sewing quilt squares, making corn husk dolls, and more. In 2007, the Riley's Lockhouse Program received the national Take Pride in America award from the US Department of the Interior. The program also won the 2007 George B. Hartzog Jr. Award for outstanding volunteer youth group in the local national capital region. (Below, courtesy Graydon Moss.)

Since 1993, the Smithsonian's National Air and Space Museum has held an annual open house for Girl Scouts at either the National Mall or its Udvar-Hazy Center in Chantilly, Virginia. Girls can see a Space Shuttle up close, take the controls of a flight simulator, and learn how things fly.

Girl Scouts can also meet female scientists, astronauts, and military pilots. The event provides many opportunities to promote STEM (science, technology, engineering, and mathematics) careers for girls. Perhaps these Daisies will grow up to become Air Force pilots.

Since 1999, Camp CEO has paired Senior and Ambassador Girl Scouts with high-powered women executives for a week of camping, bonding, and leadership development. In 2004, Camp CEO was held at Camp Coles Trip in Stafford, Virginia.

The women executives come from a range of career paths, including banking, law, real estate, academic, and government, even Girl Scouting. GSCNC CEO Lidia Soto-Harmon (center) is always the first to register for the event.

Girl Scout Seniors from Troop No. 384 in Springfield, Virginia, did a container garden for their Take Action Project for their "Sow What?" Journey. The girls prepared the container by researching the soil and types of vegetables to grow. They made a schedule and took turns watering, weeding, repairing the deer fence and harvesting over the summer. The girls donated the vegetables each week to the church where they meet for it to use in its ministries, including Rising Hope. They harvested peppers, zucchini, tomatoes, carrots, and one eggplant.

GEICO sponsored the DASHboard Road Safety patch program for teen Girl Scouts. The workshops combined real-world science with critical thinking and life skills. Girls learned how cars work, the basics of car care, and the dangers of texting while driving, so they are ready to be responsible drivers. In 2013, GEICO partnered with the council on a Practical Life Skills Challenge.

Girls get the "scoop" on the world of journalism at the annual Girl Scout Day at the Newseum, a Washington-based museum that chronicles centuries of news stories and the power of free speech and free press. A panel of women journalists shared the ups and downs of a career in the news. The Newseum also hosted a sleepover for hundreds of Girl Scouts in town for the Rock the Mall celebration in June 2012.

Encuentro de Chicas Latinas is an annual conference that introduces teen Latinas to Girl Scouts and helps them realize their leadership potential. The three-day experience includes workshops on business, public speaking, self-esteem, and college preparedness, mixed with camping, high-adventure sports, and guest speakers. Over 2,000 girls have attended an Encuentro since the program began in 2005.

Seven

THE NATION'S CAPITAL

Living in and around Washington, DC, brings a wealth of unique opportunities for the Girl Scouts of the Nation's Capital. Troops can play tourist, visiting the many area museums as regular guests, or they can sign up for special programming offered just for Girl Scouts. But they also have many unique opportunities that come from living in close proximity to the seat of the US government.

Each year, the Girl Scout Council of the Nation's Capital receives requests from local and national organizations and governmental agencies for Girl Scouts to perform duties such as flag ceremonies, help at receptions and special events, and speak with media about the opportunities available to all Girl Scouts. Troops may sign up for the Sudden Service program to take part in these often prestigious and limited-access events. These requests—often made at the last minute—may ask for a specific number of girls or a particular age group. Troops must make sure their uniforms are clean and pressed, with correctly placed insignia, so they can be ready at a moment's notice. These Girl Scouts may find themselves welcoming foreign heads of state or posing for a photograph opportunity at the Smithsonian Institution. They also host Girl Scouts and Girl Guides from around the world.

Generations of Girl Scouts have headed to the White House in the spring to take part in the annual Easter Egg Roll. Officially, the girls are there to work—rounding up lost children, leading games, demonstrating egg rolling techniques, and giving directions. But the girls themselves have a blast, greeting celebrities and brushing elbows with the first family. One year, First Lady Grace Coolidge brought girls into the White House to meet her pet raccoon, and another time she gave each member of Washington's Troop No. 12 a red rose from the Rose Garden, as that flower was their troop crest.

Every four years, Girl Scouts head to Capitol Hill or Pennsylvania Avenue to take part in the presidential inauguration. In 1917, parade organizers were not sure girls would be up to the long march, so they had 400 Girl Scouts come out to the Ellipse several days early to drill. The girls passed with flying colors and have marched in every inaugural parade since. In late 2008, Washington-area Girl Scouts and Boy Scouts were invited to tour the newly opened Capitol Visitor Center and to take a peek at the preparations for Pres. Barack Obama's swearing in. Two years later, Nation's Capital, GSUSA, and the Congressional Black Caucus hosted a milk-and-cookies reception to launch the new African Americans in Congress patch program, which teaches about the civil rights movement and advocacy.

Americans come together at the National Mall in Washington, DC, and Girl Scouts are no exception. Troops can work on badges in the sciences, fine arts, and history by visiting the free museums of the Smithsonian Institution, and Seniors and Ambassadors can lead tours as docents at the National Portrait Gallery. The Smithsonian National Zoo hosts the annual celebration of the top cookie sellers as well as the Scout Snooze at the Zoo, an overnight campout.

Nation's Capital celebrated the 75th anniversary of Girl Scouts on the National Mall on April 26, 1987. Over 80,000 Girl Scouts, their friends, and their families enjoyed a day packed with activities, including skill demonstrations, singing, dancing, a career exploration tent, history displays, and an enormous closing ceremony.

Building on that experience, Nation's Capital invited all their Girl Scout friends to return to the National Mall to celebrate subsequent milestones in the Girl Scout movement. Enormous sing-a-longs were held for the 85th, 90th, and 95th birthdays, culminating in the 100th birthday in 2012, when a quarter million Girl Scouts came to Rock the Mall.

In 1938, Henrietta Brooke was elected national president of Girl Scouts after serving many years as president of the Girl Scouts of the District of Columbia. When she sent New Year's greetings to all Girl Scouts on January 1, 1939, she included the following special section for girls in her own council:

> You form an important part of a great family of over half a million Girl Scouts. Your banners must be carried high and valiantly for you are looked to for leadership by the whole organization.
>
> The Girl Scouts of the Nation's Capital must serve as an inspiration and an example of high accomplishment. You have a double opportunity to serve Scouting and your community and therefore a double responsibility.
>
> A trust has been given us all since the great growth of the Scout movement is proof that we are making a valuable contribution to citizenship.

Over 100 years have passed since Juliette Gordon Low opened the Girl Scout national headquarters in Washington, DC. Her movement has transformed from the first eight girls who made up Washington's Troop No. 1 to the 90,000 girls and adult volunteers registered with the Nation's Capital Council today. Yet the purpose and meaning and Girl Scouting have changed little—to serve God and country, to help others, and to make the world a better place.

Girl Scouts have been involved in presidential inaugural activities since Pres. Woodrow Wilson was sworn in for a second term in March 1917. The 1917 parade was the first to allow women to march. First, however, the Girl Scouts had to prove they were up to the task with a practice drill at the Ellipse on the White House grounds. They passed inspection and placed an ad in the *Washington Post* inviting "All Girl Scouts of Washington who have uniforms" to march. "No coats or sweaters will be permitted. Black shoes and stocking and white gloves are also to be worn." The day was so cold that the girls stuffed newspapers under their uniforms for extra warmth.

Hyattsville's Troop No. 11, led by Jessie Dashiell (far left), was invited to the White House for the 11th birthday of Girl Scouting, in March 1923. The girls decided to bring a gift of homemade jellies and preserves to give to Pres. Calvin Coolidge. The girls were quite surprised to discover that the president had fiery-red hair. When Bertha Warrick finished her speech and handed him the basket, the president replied, "Well, thank ya . . . thank ya, very nice, very nice, you might as well keep it, you'll want to have your picture taken with it." They let him hold it for the photograph.

More recently, Girl Scouts have served as parade ushers, helping with crowd control and offering directions. While freezing temperatures cancelled the parade for Ronald Reagan's second inauguration in 1985, the girls worked at inaugural balls, where they helped open limo doors for lucky ticket holders. Girls also worked at a pre-inaugural event at the Library of Congress, where they met actor Jimmy Stewart.

Girl Scout volunteers are always easy to spot in their commemorative hats, jackets, or vests. These girls were part of the crew for President Obama's second swearing-in on January 21, 2013. Over 1,500 Girl Scouts and Boy Scouts participated in inaugural events, giving them an inside look at the political process and making them eyewitnesses to history.

King George VI and Queen Elizabeth reviewed 13,000 Girl and Boy Scouts lined up along the White House driveway as the royals departed for a garden party at the British Embassy on June 10, 1939. When Leah Burket of Linden, Maryland, stepped forward to present a bouquet to the queen, Her Majesty paused the procession for a closer look at one of Leah's medals. The king seems quite interested, too.

Troop No. 56 from Prince George's County lays a wreath at the Jefferson Memorial on April 13, 1952, the 209th birthday of the third president of the United States. Some 10,000 citizens came for the hour-long Easter Sunday ceremony that was led by Pres. Harry S. Truman.

Senior Girl Scout Sonja Aldren of Troop No. 281 and Mrs. Malcolm S. Edgar, GSUSA first vice president, present Pres. John F. Kennedy with a bouquet of roses for his wife on March 16, 1961. Ellen Horton of Troop No. 776 (not shown) also gave him a Brownie doll for his daughter.

One hundred twenty-five Senior Girl Scouts from across the country came to debate current events in Washington at "Petticoats, Pot, and Politics" from June 25–July 4, 1972. Among the many issues discussed, the girls concluded that marijuana possession should be reduced to a misdemeanor offense. They stayed at Trinity College and culminated their week by meeting Julie Nixon Eisenhower, daughter of Pres. Richard M. Nixon, at a White House reception. The Julie Eisenhower Fund granted Nation's Capital funds to recruit leaders for troops in low-income areas in 1971–1972.

GSUSA held its 40th National Council Session in Washington in October 1975. Over 20,000 Girl Scouts and their families presented honorary president and First Lady Betty Ford, right, with a special bicentennial gift—a book of projects and pledges from girls across the country to make the United States a better place to live. "You have adjusted to the times with creativity," Betty Ford commented. "You have changed and no doubt continue to change." Local troops helped with the opening ceremony (above).

Girl Scouts have been regular volunteers at the annual White House Easter Egg Roll since the 1920s. The girls play games with the children and provide a sense of comfort for any lost children until they are reunited with their families.

Newly invested as national honorary president, First Lady Nancy Reagan receives a bouquet from Brownie Rhonda Johnson on May 15, 1981. Local Girl Scouts have been privileged to attend a variety of functions at the White House over the years.

Local Girl Scouts present First Lady Hillary Rodham Clinton with copies of the new "Girl Scouts Against Smoking" booklets and patch, along with a new Junior sash in 1997. A former Girl Scout herself, Clinton warmly welcomed Girl Scouts to the State Department during her tenure as US secretary of state.

Many teens felt inspired and privileged to meet former secretary of state Madeleine Albright, who is a former Girl Scout herself. All three of the female secretaries of state, including Hillary Rodham Clinton and Condoleezza Rice, are Girl Scout alumnae.

From Daisies to Ambassadors, over 400 Girl Scouts from the Washington area joined First Lady Michelle Obama on the White House lawn in October 2011; their goal was to set the world record for the highest number of jumping jacks.

Girl Scouts from the Nation's Capital had the privilege of being in the Oval Office on October 29, 2009, when President Obama signed the Girl Scouts of the USA Commemorative Coin Act, which authorized the minting of 350,000 silver dollar coins. First Lady and honorary GSUSA president Michelle Obama, right, looks on.

Junior Troop No. 5869 from Rockville, Maryland, attended the October 2012 US Patent and Trademark Office (PTO) Expo. The day's activities included a scavenger hunt, trademarked characters, an intellectual property patch workshop, and a visit to the American Girl exhibit. The best part, according to the girls, was learning the difference between a patent and a trademark from actual PTO employees.

For years, troops visiting the Washington, DC, area earned the Discover the Nation's Capital patch, which led them on a scavenger hunt through the capital's museums and monuments. One favorite stop is the National Portrait Gallery, which has the 1887 oil portrait of Juliette Gordon Low by Edward Hughes.

Girl Scouts love to sing. They sing during ceremonies, hiking on trails, before meals, around the campfire, and during camp announcements. Singing is a great way to connect, as girls from across the country find they know the same songs, and mothers hear their daughters singing the same tunes they learned at camp years ago. So what better way to celebrate a birthday than with a sing-a-long? Girl Scouts from across the globe gathered on the National Mall in Washington, DC, to celebrate the movement's milestones. They came for the 85th birthday in 1997, the 90th in 2002, and the 95th in 2007.

For the 100th birthday of Girl Scouts, Washington and the Nation's Capital Council played host to Girl Scouts from around the world. Getting ready to Rock the Mall are, from left to right, Nation's Capital president Diane Tipton, Nation's Capital CEO Lidia Soto-Harmon, GSUSA president Connie Lindsey, and GSUSA CEO Anna Maria Chávez.

On June 9, 2012, over 250,000 Girl Scouts came together at the National Mall in Washington, DC. The day marked the centennial of Girl Scouting with Rock the Mall, a huge concert, a fashion show of old uniforms, SWAPS, vendors, food, and more. As the movement soars into its second century, Girl Scouts of the Nation's Capital will be there.

DISCOVER THOUSANDS OF LOCAL HISTORY BOOKS FEATURING MILLIONS OF VINTAGE IMAGES

Arcadia Publishing, the leading local history publisher in the United States, is committed to making history accessible and meaningful through publishing books that celebrate and preserve the heritage of America's people and places.

Find more books like this at
www.arcadiapublishing.com

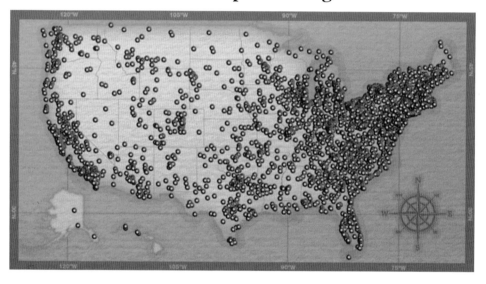

Search for your hometown history, your old stomping grounds, and even your favorite sports team.

Consistent with our mission to preserve history on a local level, this book was printed in South Carolina on American-made paper and manufactured entirely in the United States. Products carrying the accredited Forest Stewardship Council (FSC) label are printed on 100 percent FSC-certified paper.

MADE IN THE USA